THE
DEADLIEST
MONSTER

an introduction to worldviews

J.F. BALDWIN

Worldview Academy
P.O. Box 310106
New Braunfels, TX 78131
www.worldview.org

THE DEADLIEST MONSTER
Published by Fishermen Press
ISBN #0-9663176-0-2

©1998 by J.F. Baldwin
second printing, 2001
third printing, 2003
fourth printing, 2005

Cover design by Jeff Stoddard

For information:

Worldview Academy
P.O. Box 310106
New Braunfels, TX 78131
(830) 620-5203
www.worldview.org

To True and Kate,
my two favorite little monsters.

J.F. BALDWIN

WORLDVIEW ACADEMY

Worldview Academy is a non-denominational Christian camping and resource ministry com mitted to help Christians think and live in accord with their worldview. Toward this end, WVA offers week-long camps nation-wide—everywhere from Washington state to the East Coast—for students 13 and older. Although most programs treat students like "fun-junkies," Worldview Academy treats students like real people who wrestle with tough issues. Students at a WVA Leadership Camp spend about 26 hours in class, learning to "take captive every thought to make it obedient to Christ" (2 Corinthians 10:5). They graduate with a basic understanding of non-Christian worldviews like the New Age movement and Islam, and the ability to apply the Christian worldview to fundamental questions about origins, aesthetics, and human nature.

Classes integrate to form a foundation in three key areas: worldview, apologetics/evangelism, and leadership. In addition, students apply what they've learned in various practicums, so that they leave the camp with both head-knowledge and heart-knowledge.

To receive a brochure and registration form, call 800-241-1123.

ACKNOWLEDGMENTS

I used to believe that writing non-fiction was easier than writing fiction, but that was before I had to write any acknowledgments. It's hard to know what to do here. In some ways, this page wouldn't be complete unless I listed almost everyone I know, because most people I meet have taught me something about their worldview or mine (or both). In another sense, I feel like only one name belongs here— Linda, my ever-graceful wife—because she, of course, did most of the day-to-day supporting and encouraging, and because she reveres my writing far beyond all bounds of taste or common sense.

Still, some friends stand out dramatically. Briant McKellips believed in my writing almost as fervently as Linda, even way back in high school. Thanks for your incredible loyalty, Pointer. Scott Myers models the Christian walk for me every day, and makes me proud to be his friend. Todd Kent and Randy Sims put up with an awful lot of talking and dreaming, and they stay in the harness so I can do frivolous things like write books. Bill Jack taught me much of what I know about worldviews and, more importantly, taught me that attitude and actions speak louder than words. The same could be said for Jay Butler, who provided valuable suggestions for this manuscript. Kevin Bywater shared his vast knowledge of pseudo-Christian cults. And Don Miller really *wanted* this book, which is a refreshing attitude considering how most publishers respond to unknown writers.

The person most responsible for this book, though, defies description. She eats baked potatoes cold like apples, she recently broke her front teeth in a mountain biking accident, and she pickets abortion clinics relentlessly. She is my mom. And thanks to her patient love and discipline, I learned exactly what kind of monster I am.

CONTENTS

J.F. BALDWIN

PROLOGUE

Mad Scientists

Twice upon a time, there lived two scientists who became obsessed with an idea. The first scientist—later described as a "mad" scientist—was obsessed with separating his good side from his bad side. The second scientist, also slandered as mad, was obsessed with creating life from non-life.

And so both scientists set out, in their own way, to fulfill their obsession—and both succeeded, with disastrous results.

The names of these two scientists are as familiar, and haunting, as the bogeyman under your bed, but their stories have become jumbled in a swirling cycle of black and white movies and Bugs Bunny cartoons. To understand the monsters they created, we must remember the stories of Dr. Henry Jekyll and Dr. Victor Frankenstein.

Dr. Jekyll entered the world with everything a person could want: "I was born in the year 18-- to a large fortune, endowed besides with excellent parts, inclined by nature to industry, fond of the respect of the wise and good among my fellowmen, and thus, as might have been supposed, with every guarantee of an honourable and distinguished future."[1] And indeed his future was bright: he matured into a daring scientist, willing to experiment with possibilities that most men would not even consider. He numbered among his friends some of the most respectable men in London, including a prominent lawyer named Utterson.

Unfortunately, Jekyll also seemed to count among his friends a certain Edward Hyde. This small, twisted man with a penchant for absurdly large clothing somehow haunted Jekyll, never appearing with him but always appearing to be close to him. When Mr. Utterson meets Mr. Hyde, he is disgusted by the little man—almost physically ill at the sight of this monster. Recalling the meeting, Utterson mourns for Dr. Jekyll: "[I]f ever I read Satan's signature upon a face, it is on that of your new friend."[2] And this horrible recognition causes Utterson to do what his exaggerated discretion would not normally allow him to do—confront Jekyll about his friend.

The confrontation does not go well. Jekyll begins the discussion relaxed, but he quickly grows uneasy as the subject of Hyde is broached. At the close of this confrontation Jekyll, in his own kindly way, seeks to reassure Utterson: "[J]ust to put your good heart at rest, I will tell you one thing: the moment I choose, I can be rid of Mr. Hyde. I give you my hand upon that . . ."[3]

But the world was not so easily rid of Hyde. The monster came out roaring a year later and viciously beat to death a member of Parliament. The whole scene was witnessed by a maid and the hunt for Hyde was on in earnest.

Though Utterson did not want to upset Jekyll again, he knew that he must ask him the whereabouts of Hyde. Jekyll's response was typically mysterious: he produced a letter written by Hyde in which the monster guarantees that he is disappearing forever. "I swear to God," Jekyll desperately promised, "I will never set eyes on him again. I bind my honour to you that I am done with him in this world."[4]

Jekyll should have said *undone*. Try as he might, he cannot rid himself of Hyde, and eventually the monster destroys him. The story of Hyde ends with Utterson and a butler breaking into Jekyll's lab and finding that Hyde has just committed suicide—but it is precisely here that Dr. Jekyll's whole story comes to light.

Near the body of Hyde, Utterson finds Jekyll's "confession," and as he reads, he finds that the truth is almost more than he can bear: the monster Hyde is the kindly Jekyll! By means of a potion, Dr. Henry Jekyll could transform himself into evil Edward Hyde, and then drink the same potion and revert into Jekyll. The division, Jekyll claimed, was quite natural:

> I was no more myself when I laid aside restraint and plunged in shame, than when I laboured, in the eye of day, at the furtherance of knowledge or the relief of sorrow and suffering. . . . With every day, and from both sides of my intelligence, the moral and the intellectual, I thus drew steadily nearer to that truth, by whose partial discovery I have been doomed to such a dreadful shipwreck: that man is not truly one, but truly two.[5]

"A house divided against itself will not stand"—how much harder, then, for one man engaged in a power struggle with himself. At the beginning of the experiment, Jekyll was in control, and he assumed that as creator of the monster he would remain in control. He was wrong. Gradually, the transformation from Jekyll to Hyde became easier and easier, and the transformation back to his good side became more and more painful. Soon Hyde could take over Jekyll without the aid of the potion. Hyde's tragic end represents Jekyll's last gasp—the good scientist found himself at last completely trapped in Hyde's persona, unable even with the aid of the potion to revert to normal—and he chose suicide rather than enslavement to his monster.

Jekyll's experiment had succeeded—too well.

D R . F R A N K E N S T E I N

Dr. Victor Frankenstein's experiment also produced a monster, and this monster, too, was very much like a man. After years of study, Frankenstein compiled the parts of various corpses and gave them the spark of life, creating his monster. This monster was grotesquely large, and so hideous that Dr. Frankenstein fled from his creation as soon as it came to life. For about two years, the scientist saw and heard nothing of his golem.

That peaceful time shattered when the scientist's seven-year-old brother was murdered. Though a family friend was charged with the murder, Frankenstein felt instinctively that his brother's real murderer was his monster. Unable to convince authorities of the family friend's innocence, Frankenstein saw her unjustly hanged for murder.

Mourning during a sojourn in the mountains, Frankenstein was astounded to meet his creation. In his defense, the monster told a tragic tale: wherever he turned, he found himself shunned by men. He concluded that this rejection was based on his inability to communicate, and so he busied himself learning to read and speak the language. He also performed good deeds, chopping firewood in secret for a family, and even rescuing a young woman from drowning in a river. In these ways, he hoped to show the world that he was good and worthy of friendship. The monster was so pure, in fact, that he claims that

> For a long time I could not conceive how one
> man could go forth to murder his fellow, or
> even why there were laws and governments;
> but when I heard details of vice and bloodshed,
> my wonder ceased and I turned away with
> disgust and loathing.[6]

This innocence, however, was short-lived. Although the monster learned the language and lived a good life, men still hated and rejected him. The last straw, it seems, occurred when the monster rescued the young woman and, as he carried her to safety, was shot in the shoulder by the woman's fiancé.

> This was then the reward of my benevolence! I
> had saved a human being from destruction,
> and as a recompense I now writhed under the
> miserable pain of a wound which shattered the
> flesh and bone. The feelings of kindness and
> gentleness which I had entertained but a few
> moments before gave place to hellish rage and
> gnashing of teeth. Inflamed by pain, I vowed
> eternal hatred and vengeance to all mankind.[7]

As Dr. Frankenstein suspected, his creation wreaked vengeance on his little brother first. Frankenstein is faced with only one way to appease the monster: to create another, a mate, that will respond to the monster in love. According to the murderous wretch, if one being loved him, "for that one creature's sake I would make peace with the whole kind!"[8]

Though it seemed unwise, Dr. Frankenstein agrees to create a companion for his first creation, and he travels to a remote and barren part of Scotland to begin his work. As he ponders his work, however, he realizes that a second creation would only multiply the world's troubles, and he chooses to destroy the beginnings of the second monster. His destruction is intruded upon by his first monster, who flies into a rage and promises to exact revenge on Dr. Frankenstein's own wedding night.

It is at this point that our scientist comes closest to being mad. In spite of the monster's warning, in spite of his recent discovery that his closest friend has been murdered, Frankenstein goes through with his plans to marry his lifelong love. Predictably, as he checks to make sure their honeymoon home is secure, Frankenstein hears the screams of his beloved as she is killed by his monster. This horrible sequence drives the scientist to despair, and he vows to pursue his monster to the end of the world, and destroy him.

He almost makes good on his promise. The end of the story finds the monster in the frozen arctic using a dogsled to stay one step ahead of Dr. Frankenstein. The exhausted scientist is rescued by the captain of an expedition ship, and it is this captain who hears the "confession" of the monster's creator.

The story of Frankenstein ends as the story of Jekyll ends: with the death of the scientist. And yet it is not so tidy; we do not witness the monster's death, only his disappearance over the dark arctic horizon. The reader is left to wonder: did the monster kill himself, as he promised he would, or does he still roam the earth today, angry and bloodthirsty?

At this point, one might be tempted to respond with a yawn. Who cares? The story of the monster of Frankenstein is just that, a story, and no such monsters haunt us here. Both *Frankenstein* and *Dr. Jekyll and Mr. Hyde* are simply scary novels written a long time ago—why bother with them?

This attitude, though, assumes that all stories are false—and that's not a safe assumption to make. As it happens, one of these stories is true . . .

"I thought I should at least find many companions in my study of man, since it is his true and proper study. I was wrong. Even fewer people study man than mathematics."

—Blaise Pascal

CHAPTER 1

THE MONSTER IN THE MIRROR

Everyone says that it's time to stop believing in monsters. Ghosts, werewolves, and vampires exist only in your imagination—grow up! There's no mummy in your closet, and those sounds from the basement are the water pipes. Everyone says they don't believe in monsters—but they do.

Every thinking person in the world believes firmly that *either* the story of Frankenstein or the story of Jekyll and Hyde is true. It's just that we can't agree about which one it is.

What's more, it matters who is right and who is wrong. If Hyde walks the earth, we'd better be ready; if it's the monster of Frankenstein, we should act accordingly. But honest people on both sides swear vehemently that they know the truth and that the other side is wrong.

Which side do you choose? It's no use saying that you're neutral, that you haven't seen either of the monsters. Whether you're looking on the streets of London or on the arctic tundra, you're looking in the wrong place. There's only one place you can expect to get a good glimpse: your mirror.

What kind of monster are you? When you look in the mirror and when you look in your heart, what do you find? Are you more like the monster of Frankenstein, or Jekyll and Hyde?

People don't really believe that there's one certain Hyde prowling the streets or one certain animated cadaver mushing around on a dogsled. But they do believe that either the story of Frankenstein or the story of Jekyll is the story of themselves, and of Everyman. They either believe that the monster of Frankenstein speaks for them when he says, "I was benevolent and good; misery made me a fiend. Make me happy, and I shall again be virtuous,"[2] or they believe Jekyll speaks for them when he says, "It was the curse of mankind that these incongruous [personalities—the good and the bad] were thus bound together—that in the agonised womb of consciousness, these polar twins should be continuously struggling."[3]

Either Mary Shelley wrote the story of Everyman in *Frankenstein*, or Robert Louis Stevenson wrote it in *Dr. Jekyll and Mr. Hyde*. They could not both have written it, because there are no two monsters more different than their creations.

What kind of monster are you? The way you answer this question forms the foundation for your beliefs about all of reality—your religion, your *worldview*. And if you've been conscious of your existence for more than two minutes, you've already answered it, at least in its more typical formulation: What is the nature of man?

Answer this question the wrong way, and you ensure that you will adhere to a false religion, whether it be Buddhism, atheism, Islam, or any other. Lay the wrong foundation, and whatever edifice you build on it, it will totter and crumble. False religions cannot endure scrutiny because their underlying assumptions undermine them, no matter how intricate or durable they may appear.

Answer this question the right way, and you almost certainly will find yourself in a ragged, funny herd, following the Way, the Truth and the Life.

The question matters: What is the nature of man?

Consider first how the story of Frankenstein answers the question. When the monster is "born," he is pure and innocent—he can't understand why men have governments, because he can't imagine why anyone would do anything immoral or illegal. Unfortunately, society does not treat the monster well. They shun him because he is ugly, and even when he responds in love they mistreat him. Finally, his environment twists his good impulses and he responds in rage. He excuses his actions by pointing out, "Am I to be thought the only criminal, when all humankind sinned against me?"[4]

The story of Dr. Jekyll is just the opposite. Though Jekyll is born into an environment that should be perfectly conducive to good behavior, he still has the tendency to choose to do wrong. Once he recognizes this tendency, he seeks to use science to separate his twin desires—so that he can be perfectly good some of the time, and "perfectly" bad some of the time. Thanks to a potion, he succeeds at allowing his evil tendencies to run amok in the form of Mr. Hyde, but he finds that he is still not perfectly good as Dr. Jekyll:

> Hence, although I had now two characters as
> well as two appearances, one was wholly evil,
> and the other was still the old Henry Jekyll,
> that incongruous compound of whose reforma-
> tion and improvement I had already learned to
> despair. The movement was thus wholly
> toward the worse.[5]

What's more, Jekyll finds that by unleashing his bad side he has allowed it to slowly take over his life, leading to murder and ultimately to suicide. And he has no one to blame for these bad turns but himself.

Only one of these monsters lives our story. Man cannot be both like the monster of Frankenstein and like Jekyll and Hyde. Which one is he?

THE CHRISTIAN MONSTER

You won't receive any hints from the authors of the stories—both Stevenson and Shelley were what may best be described as "modern pagans." Both rejected the God of the Bible and were unscrupulous about breaking up marriages in pursuit of love. Both would be expected to describe the nature of man in the same way. But only one was, as G.K. Chesterton noticed, "a Christian theologian without knowing it:"[6] Robert Louis Stevenson.

Christians, if they are at all consistent with their faith, should demand loudly that man is like Jekyll and Hyde. They recognize, as Socrates did, that "the ruling power in us men drives a pair of horses, and . . . one of these horses is fine and good and of noble stock, and the other the opposite in every way. So in our case the task of the charioteer is necessarily a difficult and unpleasant business."[7] In other words, man is divided against himself: he "knows the good he ought to do and doesn't do it" (James 4:17). We are sinful creatures, every one of us, and though we think we have good impulses we cannot obey them for an hour—let alone a day.[8]

Further, the Bible makes it clear that we are destined to become enslaved by our sinful side, because we must be either slaves to sin or slaves to righteousness (Romans 6:16-18). Since we are unable to be righteous, we find ourselves more and more controlled by our Hyde, until he has taken over our life. Sin, given even the faintest toe-hold, will make a suicide of us.

The story of Dr. Jekyll and Mr. Hyde is uncannily like the biblical description of unredeemed man. We are born with the seed of sin planted in us by Adam (Romans 5:12); we know what is right but we refuse to do it (Romans 1:18-20); we want to let our own little pet sins lead us for awhile and then get back in control, but instead we find these sins controlling us (Romans 7:22-24); and then man finds, too late, that "the wages of sin is death" (Romans 6:23).

Unredeemed man, like Jekyll and Hyde, is a horror story. We are separated from God from the beginning, and as our sin matures we distance ourselves from our only hope more and more. *Nothing* we do can save us; we will live and die as Jekyll lived and died—unless.

And this "unless" contains all the hope and all the joy in all of heaven. We cannot be saved *unless* the very God that we have been separate from since birth and that we rebel against every day offers Himself as a living sacrifice for our sins on the cross! And then by trusting Him to rescue us—understanding that nothing we do saves us—we find our Hyde nailed on the cross with Him, and we are born again.

The story of *Dr. Jekyll and Mr. Hyde* is true, and it matters very much that it is true. Until we believe it—with all its horror and all its bad news—we will never be ready to receive the good news: the gospel of Jesus Christ. Until we recognize that we are sinners desperately in need of a Savior, we won't begin our frantic search for that Savior. You've got to know you're hopelessly lost before you start shouting to be found.

The Frankenstein Crowd

The Frankenstein crowd—those who believe that the story of Frankenstein is actually the true story—believe in an entirely different bit of "good news." They believe that man—any man and every man—is basically good. They believe that we need not cast about for a Savior because we're good enough to work out our own salvation.[9] These people conclude (logically, if their assumption is correct) that they don't need Jesus Christ to die for them. They can fix what's wrong themselves.

Cultural leaders express this sentiment all the time. Carl Rogers, one of the most influential psychologists of the 20th century, writes, "For myself, though I am very well aware of the incredible amount of destructive, cruel, malevolent behavior in today's world—from the threats of war to the senseless violence in the streets—I do not find that this evil is inherent in human nature."[10] Abraham Maslow, a psychologist who may have had even more influence than Rogers on modern culture, says that "As far as I know we just don't have any intrinsic instincts for evil."[11] Aldous Huxley, the author of *Brave New World*, says "It is because we don't know Who we are, because we are unaware that the Kingdom of Heaven is within us, that we behave in the generally silly, the often insane, the sometimes criminal ways that are so characteristically human. We are saved, we are liberated and enlightened, by perceiving the hitherto unperceived good that is already within us . . ."[12]

This attitude is then summarized by the men and women who signed the second *Humanist Manifesto*: "While there is much that we do not know, humans are responsible for what we are or will become. No deity will save us; we must save ourselves."[13]

This attitude reflects the belief that the story of Frankenstein is the story of Everyman. Remember, the monster of Frankenstein was a basically good monster. He couldn't understand why men behaved badly, and all he wanted was for other men to treat him well. He acted altruistically—working to meet others' needs by chopping firewood. And then, finally, as a result of bad environmental influences, the good monster went bad—but his bad behavior was not his fault. The world that shunned him was responsible.

Strange to say, virtually every non-Christian believes that the story of Frankenstein is his story. Though this belief is diametrically opposed to the Christian view of the nature of man, and though you might expect some non-Christians to believe something at least slightly more akin to the Christian view, almost every person who is not a Christian avows man's basic goodness. What kind of monster is man? Man is Frankenstein, non-Christians say—basically good and certainly capable of working out his own salvation.

It might be helpful at this point to discard a piece of baggage that almost certainly is riding around the conveyor belt in your brain. If you're like most people, you tend to think of religions along a spectrum—that is, you imagine atheism at one end of a line, and Christianity at the other end. Those religions similar to atheism, like agnosticism and animism, occur pretty close to the endpoint (atheism), but are a bit nearer to Christianity. Nearer still occur religions like the New Age movement, Buddhism and Hinduism. Quite close to Christianity you might find monotheistic religions like Islam and Judaism, and even closer various pseudo-Christian cults like the Jehovah's Witnesses and Mormons. This imaginary spectrum reflects the belief that some religions are very dissimilar to Christianity, and that others are very similar. And in one way, this belief is right.

It's true that some religions attack almost everything about orthodox Christianity, and other religions say that they agree almost completely with Christianity. Some religions even adopt the outward forms and much of the language of the Christian faith. And so it seems logical to conclude that the Jehovah's Witness is much closer to Christianity than is the atheist.

But this assumption, as we've said, is baggage we had best discard. Though many religions *outwardly* appear similar to Christianity, they are as fundamentally different from Christianity as pleading innocent is from pleading guilty. No other worldview can possibly accept the Christian contention that man is a desperate sinner who can do nothing to save himself. *Every* other worldview—including Islam, including Mormonism—believes, at bottom, that man—if not perfect—is at least "good enough" to save himself.

You might find this hard to swallow. Islam speaks of sin, as does Mormonism—and certainly Jews believe that man is a sinner. Why would anyone lump all of these religions in with the Frankenstein crowd?

Why? Because they fit. Is there any other religion that says to man what Paul says in Ephesians 2:8-9: "For it is by grace you have been saved, through faith—and this not from yourselves, it is the gift of God—not by works, so that no one can boast."? Does any other religion tell man that he is so rebellious that none of his works will save him?

Jesus tells a parable about two men who went to the temple to pray. One, a Pharisee, stood up and thanked God that he was not really that sinful, like robbers or tax collectors. He bragged about his works, reminding God that he fasted twice a week and tithed consistently. The second man, a tax collector, dared not even look up to heaven. He prayed simply, "God, have mercy on me, a sinner." Jesus tells us that the tax collector and not the Pharisee "went home justified before God" (Luke 18:9-14). Perhaps better than any other parable, this highlights the difference between Christians and the world. Christians recognize the horror story of sin, and humbly seek mercy. The world—regardless of religion— believes that their works redeem them.

This will become more obvious as this chapter progresses, as we discuss the beliefs of the ten most influential non-Christian religions, including their foundational faith about the nature of man. This brief survey will underscore the fact that every false religion aligns itself with the Frankenstein crowd.

For now, simply discard the old idea of the spectrum of religions, and replace it with a new concept: a spectrum of *false* religions. Yes, all non-Christian religions can be sketched out on a spectrum ranging from atheism to monotheism—but Christianity falls nowhere near that spectrum. The Christian view of the world, and indeed of all reality, is radically different than every other view of the world. Because we start with the bad news of Hyde, we avoid all the bad logic of the Franken-stein crowd.

THE MEANING OF LIFE

Now, too, you may want to pause to recognize that you are at the starting point for your religion, your *worldview*. By answering the question, What kind of monster are you? (more accurately, What is the nature of man?), you have made the first assumption upon which all your other assumptions and conclusions are based. And before you go much further, you'll notice that your first assumption leads you quite logically to answer the only other foundational question: What is the nature of God?

If you are a member of the Hyde crowd, you may respond in only one way that makes life worth living: God must be that perfect, just, and holy Person Who is also so gracious that He sacrificed His Son for us. If God is anything else, or if He does not exist, all is lost.

On the other hand, members of the Frankenstein crowd can answer this second question in a variety of ways. They may say that God does not exist and that man is the highest being; they may say that every person is a part of God; or they may say that God created the universe and then left us, and is now irrelevant. They may, in fact, say any number of things about God *except* what the Bible says: for why should they conceive of a gracious God, when man is good enough to work out his own salvation? Grace implies unmerited favor, and the Frankenstein crowd believe that man can be worthy of reward.

Everyone wants to know the meaning of life. The secret? Answer two basic questions (What is the nature of man? What is the nature of God?), and if you're right, you've found life's purpose. Even if you're wrong, every belief and every action you choose will flow naturally from your answer to those two questions—because they are the foundation for your *worldview*.

Your *worldview* is your framework for understanding existence—the way you look at the world. The terms *worldview* and *religion* are really interchangeable, when properly understood, because at bottom every worldview is based on certain faith assumptions and offers answers to the "why" questions—Why am I here? Why do I think I *ought* to do some things? Why does evil exist? etc.

Your worldview is like an invisible pair of eyeglasses—glasses you put on to help you see reality clearly. If you choose the right pair of glasses, you can see everything vividly, and can behave in sync with the real world (that is, you won't walk into walls, fall into wells, or talk to mannequins). But if you choose the wrong pair of glasses, you may find yourself in a worse plight than the blind man—thinking you see things clearly when in reality your vision is severely distorted.

Just as every thinking person has answered the monster question, every thinking person is wearing a pair of these glasses. The postman, your Aunt Lilly, Ann Landers—we all have a worldview. Men may protest that they are not religious, or that they don't have any answers about the meaning of life. But every man believes in Hyde or Frankenstein, and every man believes something about God.[14] What you believe about God and man determines what you believe about everything else.

Obviously, then, it matters what worldview you choose. If you choose Marxism, and it's true that all of reality is a clash between oppressed and oppressors, then you see reality clearly and Christians, Hindus, Muslims, and everyone else are blundering around with very little concept of what the real world looks like. But if Marxism is a false view of the world, then Christian author Barbara von der Heydt is correct in proclaiming that "The reason that Communism collapsed [in Eastern Bloc countries] is that Marxism is based on the false premise that the nature of man is inherently good and perfectible through human endeavor, that it is a product of his material surroundings, devoid of transcendence."[15] A false worldview distorts reality and dooms the plans and visions of its proponents.

Think for a moment about the people around you. It may seem that most of them are in touch with reality; that is, they know that they'll find mail in a mailbox, they can use a fork, and they don't try to fly by jumping off buildings. True, most people function quite nicely in the everyday physical world. But a closer examination shows that many people are hopelessly out of step with the most important things. How many rely on God to control their lives? How many act as though love is more important than possessions? How many bear trouble wisely and well?

Christians often flunk these tests, and we're wearing the right glasses! How then can we expect people wearing the wrong glasses to see the deepest, far-away things?

The Frankenstein crowd chooses the wrong monster and consequently puts on the wrong pair of glasses. They see a version of reality that looks more like a fun-house mirror than the real world. Their only hope? That the Holy Spirit will remove the bad glasses and cause them to "see" with the mind of Christ.

Christians can be used by the Holy Spirit in this work. We are commanded to "take captive every thought to make it obedient to Christ" (2 Corinthians 10:5)—to understand our worldview well—and also to "be prepared to give an answer to everyone who asks you to give the reason for the hope that you have" (1 Peter 3:15). Obeying these commands gives us the best opportunity to be used by God as He changes prescriptions for unredeemed men and women.

One of the very best apologetics for Christianity is the fact that it differs radically from every other version of reality, and that its differences match reality. In order to understand and articulate these differences, the Christian must understand his own worldview and the various worldviews of the Frankenstein crowd. The following survey of the ten most influential non-Christian worldviews will help you "be prepared" to fulfill the Great Commission (Matthew 28:19-20).

TEN RIVAL WORLDVIEWS

ATHEISM

People who adhere to atheism choose many different names to describe themselves: Humanist, agnostic,[16] free thinker, skeptic, naturalist, etc. All of these mean basically the same thing: these people believe that man, and all life, arose by chance natural processes. Nothing supernatural—souls, God, demons, angels, thoughts, or conscience—exists. For this reason, man becomes "master of his fate" and "captain of his soul." The self becomes the center of the universe.

Evolution, for the atheist, is much more than a hypothesis about how man came to exist. Charles Darwin's theory is exalted by the atheist to the place of "indisputable fact," because it is the only possible means of explaining creation without God. Atheists like to paint other religious people as dogmatic because these people hold to various creeds; but no religion features any creed more sacrosanct than Darwinism is for the atheist.

Because atheists view any belief in the supernatural as a delusion, they often use the modern version of "separation of church and state" to attack Christians applying their faith to the public square. Atheists claim that any theistic faith is irrational, and therefore should be allowed only to influence an individual's private life. This argument provides the theoretical foundation for the disqualification of God and Christian history from the public schools.

If the atheist is to avoid suicide, he must believe that the story of Frankenstein is true—that man is basically good. Nothing exists outside of man that could redeem him, so man's capacity for redemption must come from within. Like Frankenstein, atheists believe that it is society's fault when man does bad things, and that if you fix society you can create a utopia where all men and women do good all the time. B.F. Skinner promises that "there is no reason why progress toward a world in which people may be automatically good should be impeded."[17] Most atheists view this utopia as a one-world community, where national borders have crumbled and all men live in harmony.

Erich Fromm, an atheistic psychotherapist, flatly rejects the concept of original sin in his book *You Shall Be as Gods*: "The Christian interpretation of the story of man's act of disobedience as his 'fall' has obscured the clear meaning of the story. The biblical text does not even mention the word 'sin'; man challenges the supreme power of God, and he is able to challenge it because he is potentially God."[18]

The most coherent form of atheism is Marxism, a worldview that goes to great lengths to explain the steps by which man may rehabilitate society and create utopia. Because Marxism is so comprehensive, we will treat it as a separate worldview and discuss it shortly.

Recent prominent atheists include Charles Darwin[19], T.H.

Huxley and his grandson Julian, cable magnate Ted Turner, Margaret Sanger (founder of Planned Parenthood), psychologists B.F. Skinner and Abraham Maslow, and philosopher Bertrand Russell.

BUDDHISM

Buddhism, a worldview with roots in Hinduism, centers around the teaching of one man, Siddhartha Gautama (born around 563 B.C.).[20] Also known as "Buddha" or the "Enlightened One," Gautama came from a wealthy family and quickly grew disillusioned with worldly pursuits. He eventually deserted his wife and son to seek the meaning of life.

Buddha began his search by embracing asceticism—shunning all material comforts. This left him unfulfilled, so he began to seek a "middle way" between indulgence and self-denial. One day as he meditated under a tree, Buddha passed through a series of states of consciousness until he attained "enlightenment." This revelation led him to preach Four Noble Truths (the core doctrine of Buddhism): (1) Life is suffering. (2) Suffering is caused by desiring (specifically pleasure and other earthly concerns). (3) Suffering can be avoided by understanding reality and consequently removing one's attachment to meaningless things. (4) One may take the Noble Eightfold Path to discover the truth about reality and thereby avoid suffering. The Noble Eightfold Path consists of right views, right intention, right speech, right action, right livelihood, right effort, right-mindedness, and right contemplation.

Some Buddhists embrace the concept of reincarnation and karma, but with a unique emphasis: the individual self or soul is an illusion (we are all one), and therefore one's consciousness at death mixes with everyone else's consciousness and "reincarnates" as another "self" that may or may not contain elements of the previous individual. The idea that any man is an independent being perpetuates ignorance and should be abandoned.

There are two main "denominations" of Buddhism today: Theravada and Mahayana. Theravada Buddhists tend to put more emphasis on the sacred scriptures (the Tripitaka, or Three Baskets) and view any gods that may exist (many still believe in some of the Hindu gods) as inconsequential and mortal. Mahayana Buddhists are much more liberal in their approach to scripture, and tend to deify Buddha (granting him characteristics much like the god-force in the New Age movement). A third branch of Buddhism that originated in China, Zen, is growing in popularity in the West.

The ultimate goal for each of these branches of Buddhism is *nirvana*, a blending with the oneness of all reality that frees us from suffering caused by ignorance and desire. In keeping with the Frankenstein crowd's beliefs about the basic goodness of man, the Buddhist believes that man can achieve nirvana through his own efforts. The only thing that keeps man from getting in touch with nirvana is the illusory self, which causes him to desire and suffer. Achieving nirvana requires intense inward focus and self-contemplation, which explains the Buddhist's fascination with monasteries and hermitages.

HINDUISM

"Hinduism" is a western name originally used to describe the religion of the country of India.[21] For this reason, and because Hinduism focuses on experience more than logic, the

Hindu worldview is difficult to define. Some Hindus tend toward polytheism, worshipping numerous gods including a creator (Brahma), a destroyer (Siva), and a protector (Vishnu). In general, however, most Hindus believe these gods emanate from the "universal soul," and therefore they embrace pantheism (the belief that everything is god). This majority of Hindus expects the illusory material world to vanish and everything to be unified into that soul.

Certain beliefs are basic to every version of Hinduism. Most importantly, the orthodox Hindu believes that the Vedas (a collection of hymns, stories, and incantations) are sacred scripture—although he may treat other writings as equally sacred. Truth, for the Hindu, is not absolute—it is relative to the experience of every person. Hindus also believe in reincarnation and animism (an assumption that everything in the world is animated by spirits). Hindus use yoga and other forms of meditation in an effort to see beyond the illusion of time and space.

Man, according to this view, is capable of working out his own salvation using meditation and other occultic techniques. As the individual becomes more enlightened, he moves toward unification with the universal soul, where he will lose his individual consciousness in a collective consciousness. As with Buddhists, Hindus view the world as ultimately illusory and therefore the central obstacle to man rescuing himself.

The history of Hinduism is a history of strange and cruel superstitions. Chief among these is *suttee*, a ritual that involved burning a man's widow alive on his funeral pyre. Hindus also revere certain animals, especially the cow, and oftentimes would rather see a countryman starve than butcher that animal. In addition, Hinduism encourages a caste system based on the assumption that one's caste (social class) and sex result from one's karma from past lives. Members of different castes should not intermarry or eat together, and in the past one's caste determined one's career. Certain lower castes are viewed as unclean and even untouchable.

The New Age worldview often borrows substantially from both Hinduism and Buddhism, but it has its own Western overtones, and so we'll deal with that worldview separately.

ISLAM

Islam is one of the few monotheistic worldviews.[22] Muslims are so committed to the existence of a single, all-powerful god that they often accuse Christians of polytheism (because Christians worship a triune God).

Muslims claim that their god, Allah, is the God to which the Bible refers, but that the Bible distorts his character. The true god, they claim, is every bit as powerful as the Christian God, but he is neither as just nor as merciful as the God described in scripture. According to Islam, Allah will judge all men and allow those that please him to enter paradise (a sort of sensual pleasure palace), but there is no absolute standard by which men are judged, and there is certainly no Savior to rescue men.

Although Muslims often speak of men's actions as displeasing to Allah and recommend other actions—like praying toward Mecca and keeping the holy fasts—to please him, Muslims do not view men as sinners in the Christian sense of the word. Rather, Muslims say that individuals can and do live in a way that pleases Allah, and thus work out their own salvation. Allah need not be nearly as gracious as the God of the Bible (if, indeed, Allah is gracious at all) because men are good enough to behave in the right way if they so choose.

Hammudah Abdalati, a Muslim and a former professor of sociology at Syracuse University, flatly rejects the Jekyll and Hyde view of sin: "sin is acquired not inborn, emergent not built-in, avoidable not inevitable."[23] In fact, Muslims believe that man "is empowered by revelations, supported by reason, fortified by the freedom of choice, and guided by various social and psychological dispositions to seek and achieve relative perfection."[24] And what gets in the way of man achieving perfection? You guessed it: society.

> The idea of Original Sin or hereditary crimi-
> nality has no room in the teachings of Islam.
> Man, according to the Qur'an (30:30) and to
> the Prophet, is born in a natural state of purity
> or *fitrah*, that is, Islam or submission to the
> will and law of God. Whatever becomes of
> man after birth is the result of external influ-
> ence and intruding factors. To put the matter
> in terms of modern thought, human nature is
> malleable; it is the socialization process . . . that
> is crucial.[25]

Like Frankenstein, man starts off pure and then sees his nature twisted by his environment. But he can redeem himself by getting in touch again with his basic goodness.

Islam began in Arabia around A.D. 610, when a man named Mohammed dreamed that the angel Gabriel visited him. The angel commanded Mohammed to recite, and when he asked what he should recite, the angel replied, "Recite thou in the name of the Lord, who created man from clots of blood." In following years, Mohammed received more messages from Gabriel, ringing bells, and other media. By the time Mohammed died in 632, he claimed that he was the "Seal of the Prophets" and therefore higher than Christ, Who was merely another prophet.

Muslims believe that there were five Great Prophets who preceded Mohammed: Adam, Noah, Abraham, Moses and Jesus. Each prophet recited divine truth, but that truth was only for a time, and often became distorted as it was handed down. Muslims usually describe these prophets as "supermen"—not divine, but totally sinless. Mohammed, the greatest prophet, has revealed Allah's final word; no prophet will supplant him.

The Koran (or Qur'an), the holy book of Islam, is said to be the Word of Allah, written on a "Preserved Tablet" in heaven. This revelation was brought down piece by piece to Mohammed by the angel Gabriel over the course of 22 years. For the Muslim, the Koran supplants the Bible just as Mohammed supplants Christ.

JEHOVAH'S WITNESSES

Like Mormons, Jehovah's Witnesses (JWs) claim to adhere to the only pure form of the Christian worldview. And like Mormons, Jehovah's Witnesses distort Christian doctrine so severely that their worldview is as un-Christian as Hinduism or atheism.

The Jehovah's Witness worldview was founded by Charles Taze Russell in 1872. Though a few modern Jehovah's Wit-

THE MONSTER IN THE MIRROR

nesses deny their ties to Russell (because he demonstrated almost no integrity in his lifetime), their relationship to him becomes obvious when one studies the history of the Watchtower Bible and Tract Society (their central organization) and the blatant similarities between their doctrine and Russell's.

Among the untruths preached by Russell and accepted by Jehovah's Witnesses are: a denial of the Trinity, a belief that Christ was Michael the Archangel, an assumption that hell refers to mankind's common grave instead of eternal punishment, an assumption that only 144,000 people can enter the kingdom of heaven, and a denial of the sufficiency of the Atonement.

Jehovah's Witnesses also contradict the biblical view of the nature of man. Though Witnesses often describe man as sinful and profess that mankind needed Christ's sacrifice to help men achieve perfection, they also maintain that the individual must behave properly to ensure his own salvation. Christ's atonement, they maintain, only washed away original sin, and not the additional sin of our own bad choices and actions. Their official Bible encyclopedia, *Insight on the Scriptures*, explains:

> Jehovah God has the right to refuse to accept a
> ransom for anyone he deems unworthy.
> Christ's ransom covers the sins an individual
> has because of being a child of Adam, but a
> person can add to that by his own, deliberate,
> willful course of action, and he can thus die for
> such sin that is beyond coverage by the ran-
> som.[26]

What must man do to be saved? The Bible promises that we

are saved by grace through faith alone (Titus 3:4-7)—but Jehovah's Witnesses claim that man must be moral to ensure his salvation. They believe that only the individual is good enough to rescue himself—Christ did his best, but the rest is up to us. Their official publication, *The Watchtower*, lists four specific obligations men must fulfill to reach paradise. The first requirement is that they study the JW mistranslation of the Bible. The second?

> Many have found the second requirement more difficult. It is to *obey God's laws*, yes, to conform one's life to the moral requirements set out in the Bible . . . A third requirement is that we *be associated with God's channel*, his organization. God has always used an organization. For example, only those in the ark in Noah's day survived the Flood, and only those associated with the Christian congregation in the first century had God's favor. (Acts 4:12) Similarly, Jehovah is using only one organization today to accomplish his will [the Watchtower Bible and Tract Society]. To receive everlasting life in the earthly Paradise we must identify that organization and serve God as part of it.[27]

The fourth requirement is that the faithful must share the good news with others.

The question, of course, is, What good news? It is terribly bad news to tell the honest man that his only hope of salvation lies in obeying all of God's laws, because he realizes that he's not even capable of such perfection momentarily. And if the man unwisely believes that he is capable of perfection, then why did Christ bother to die on the cross? The whole point of Christ's sacrifice is that we were so sinful we needed a perfect blood offering (Hebrews 9:27-28). If we have the capacity to be pure, Christ's death is overkill.

The official Bible for Jehovah's Witnesses is the *New World Translation of the Holy Scriptures*, a version created by the Watchtower Society. None of the translators that created this version held legitimate degrees in Greek or Hebrew translation. As a result, this version borrows heavily from Christian translations, and usually differs from the Bible only where these Christian translations contradict Watchtower doctrine. Verses in the Bible that affirm the deity of Christ, for example, are radically altered in the *New World Translation*.

Two other characteristics prevalent among adherents to this worldview are worth noting: (1) a tendency to portray evangelicals as "enemies of God"; and (2) a history of failed prophecies. The Watchtower Society predicted that Abraham, Isaac and Jacob would return to earth before 1930, and then recently predicted that the Battle of Armageddon would occur in 1975. Despite these failures, Jehovah's Witnesses cling to the Watchtower Society as their source for divine truth.

Judaism

Traditional Judaism is the worldview most similar to Christianity, because it relies on some of the same scripture and encourages the worship of Yahweh, the one true God. There are, however, significant differences.

Based largely on the Old Testament (many Jews also rely

heavily on the Rabbinic teaching contained in the Mishnah and the Talmud), traditional Judaism teaches that God revealed His laws to man, and entered into a covenant with the nation of Israel. When Israelites uphold their end of the covenant by adhering to God's law, God blesses them and moves toward establishing them as a powerful nation. When Israelites act in a way displeasing to God, He delivers them into the hands of their enemies to remind them of their dependence upon Him. God will never entirely desert His people, but He will withdraw from them when they withdraw from Him.

Adhering to God's law requires observing numerous rites and rituals, including circumcision, abstaining from unclean foods like pork, observing the Sabbath, prayer and fasting, and animal sacrifice. Obedience tends to be more about actions than attitude.

Jews understand their worldview as comprehensive, because they recognize a supreme Creator Who reigns over the universe and directs history toward His appointed end. When God is very pleased with the nation of Israel, He will send a Messiah to rebuild His Temple in Jerusalem, rule as King, and institute a world order of justice and compassion. This order will precede the resurrection of the dead and final judgment.

Adherents to Judaism differ from Christians in that they deny the deity of Jesus Christ (consequently denying the Trinity), deny the truth of the books of the New Testament, and view salvation as a work of man in concert with the working of God. Jews ultimately fall in with the Frankenstein crowd because they believe that man is capable in some way of pleasing God and earning His favor. The book *The Jewish People: Their History and Their Religion* describes "the belief, characteristic of Judaism, that man, in his normal condition,

THE MONSTER IN THE MIRROR

inclines towards righteousness." "Moreover," the book continues, man "is not powerless to control his self-regarding drives.
To begin with, he is born untainted by sin."[28]

Rabbi David J. Wolpe, a traditional Jew, says that "Judaism
is a faith that believes in the renewal and change of the human
being. Change is hard, arduous; but it is possible. We can
remake ourselves because more than anything else, what we are
is a product of our own choice and our own work."[29] The
belief that man can "remake" himself is just another way of
saying that man can save himself, as David S. Ariel attests: "In
rabbinic thought, the purification of the human soul through
study, worship, and good deeds is the path to the world-to-
come."[30] Elsewhere Ariel nicely summarizes the Jewish attitude
toward sin: "Jewish views on sin and human nature differ significantly from those of Christianity. . . . In Christianity, sin is a fact
of birth, whereas in Judaism, sin is a matter of choice."[31]

The Jewish man or woman cannot imagine a suffering
Messiah because they are not sufficiently aware of their sinfulness to recognize that only the sacrifice of God's Son can purify
mankind.

MARXISM

Marxism, the most comprehensive atheistic worldview, is
named for its founder, Karl Marx, but owes much of its
foundation to Marx's friend and financial supporter, Frederick
Engels, and to the first leader of the Soviet Union, V.I. Lenin.
The most acceptable date for the origin of this worldview is
1848, when Marx and Engels published *The Communist
Manifesto*.

Marxist theory is based on economic determinism—a view

of history that assumes that a nation's government and all its societal institutions, and even each citizen's consciousness, are determined by the economic system of that nation. According to this view, capitalism creates a better society than feudalism, but it is still hopelessly antiquated compared to communism, the only economic system that can create the foundation for paradise. Everyone "poisoned" by the capitalist mentality must submit to (or be destroyed by) the working class, which will establish a socialistic dictatorship that will eventually evolve into communism.

Man, according to this view, is a perfectible being who only requires the right economic system to get in touch with his basic goodness. People in capitalistic societies cannot really be blamed for their actions, because their attitudes are tainted by a primitive economic system. Once worldwide communism is achieved, there will be no need for laws and governments, because everyone will freely choose to act properly all the time. At that time, each man will work according to his ability, and receive according to his needs.

Many modern radicals have "re-interpreted" Marxism to suit their own cause. Marx described the oppression of the working class by wealthier classes as the chief evil, but new radicals choose other kinds of "oppression" as the driving force behind their worldview: whites oppressing minorities, men oppressing women, heterosexuals oppressing homosexuals, etc.

Although the destruction of the Berlin Wall and the collapse of communism in the Eastern Bloc has encouraged many observers to view Marxism as "ancient history," Christians must not succumb to this temptation. More than a billion people still suffer under Marxist regimes in China,

Cuba, North Korea, and other countries.

MORMONISM

Mormons often describe themselves as Christians, but their worldview is anti-Christian in numerous ways: Mormonism adds to God's Word, denies the Trinity and original sin, preaches salvation by works, and blasphemes God by claiming that He began as nothing more than a man and evolved to His present glory.

Mormonism, or the Church of Jesus Christ of Latter-day Saints, was officially founded by Joseph Smith in 1830, though he laid the foundation for it years beforehand. Smith claimed that, when he was 14, he was visited by God and Jesus Christ, Who informed him that the modern Christian church had corrupted the truth. To re-establish true religion on earth, new revelation was necessary—revelation that was given to Smith in the form of golden plates inscribed with "reformed Egyptian." Since no one could translate "reformed Egyptian" (indeed, no credible linguist thinks such a language ever existed), Smith was provided with magic spectacles (Urim and Thummim) by the angel Moroni. These spectacles enabled Smith to translate the plates into the *Book of Mormon*.

This book, along with two other scriptures—*Doctrine and Covenants* and the *Pearl of Great Price*—are added to the Bible to derive Mormon doctrine. This doctrine is not as stable as Christian doctrine, because the Mormon church hierarchy has significantly altered portions of their sacred scripture, and may receive additional revelation at any time. The top of the hierarchy, the Council of Twelve Apostles, has a president that serves as the prophet for the Mormon church during his lifetime.

Among the practices that were once sanctioned by Mormon doctrine and have since been overturned are polygamy and racism. Until 1978, blacks were viewed as unworthy to be ordained, even though every other Mormon male could enter into the priesthood at age 12.

One Mormon dogma that has remained consistent is their belief about the nature of man. According to Mormons, man is a god-in-embryo,[32] capable of saving himself and ruling his own planet someday. As such, man is not really sinful in the Christian sense—in fact, original sin is a myth. According to M. Russell Ballard, a member of the Council of Twelve Apostles,

> The Church of Jesus Christ of Latter-day
> Saints discounts the notion of Original Sin and
> its ascribed negative impact on humanity.
> Indeed, we honor and respect Adam and Eve
> for their wisdom and foresight. Their lives in
> the Garden of Eden were blissful and pleasant;
> choosing to leave that behind so they and the
> entire human family could experience both the
> triumphs and travails of mortality must not
> have been easy. But we believe that they *did*
> choose mortality, and in so doing made it
> possible for all of us to participate in Heavenly
> Father's great, eternal plan.[33]

Jesus Christ figures somewhere in this plan, but only in a modest way:

> Because Jesus died and then conquered death

through His resurrection, all of us will have the privilege of immortality. This gift is given freely through the loving grace of Jesus Christ to all people of all ages, regardless of their good or evil acts. And to those who choose to love the Lord and who show their love and faith in Him by keeping His commandments, the Atonement offers the additional promise of exaltation, or the privilege of living in the presence of God forever.[34]

Only those who act rightly are saved, and the rest are cast into outer darkness:

At the final judgment we will be assigned to the kingdom we have earned. We will be sent to one of four places: the celestial kingdom, which is the highest degree of glory; the terrestrial kingdom, the middle degree; the telestial kingdom, which is the lowest degree of glory; outer darkness, which is the kingdom of the devil and is *not* a degree of glory.

. . . The Lord explained that our choices would earn for us one of the four kingdoms. We learn from this revelation that even members of the Church will earn different kingdoms because they will not be equally valiant in keeping the commandments.[35]

What must one do to achieve exaltation (the celestial kingdom)? Among other things, an individual must obey the

Word of Wisdom (abstaining from alcohol, caffeine, and tobacco), search out his "kindred dead" and perform the saving ordinances of the gospel for them, attend LDS meetings as regularly as possible, and conduct family and individual prayers daily. In other words, according to one of the Mormon Sunday school books, "each person must endure in faithfulness, keeping all the Lord's commandments until the end of his life on earth."[36]

Naturally, this presupposes that man is good enough to remain faithful and behave properly all of his life. Those who do so are exalted, and those who don't risk condemnation to the outer darkness.

THE NEW AGE MOVEMENT

As Solomon warns in Ecclesiastes, there is nothing new under the sun. The New Age movement is really a modern mix of the occult, eastern mysticism, and selfishness. Although New Age adherents claim that they have no dogma—that everyone creates their own truth—they all accept two basic assumptions: all is one (philosophical monism), and everything is god (pantheism).

Accepting these two premises leads to several more "truths": (1) The most important thing anyone can do is cast off all authority and live for themselves, so that they can get in touch with the god within[37]; (2) Good and evil, light and dark, male and female, etc., are all really the same thing; (3) The spirit world is our source for guidance; (4) Absolute truth does not exist; (5) Man creates his own reality, so it's our own fault when we suffer; and (6) Nobody ever dies—they just move on to a higher plane of existence or are reincarnated.

Because of its rejection of absolute truth, the New Age movement expects that there are many paths to god. Orthodox Christianity, however, cannot possibly be one of these paths, because it teaches that Christ is the only Way to God. These narrow-minded Christians, to the New Age proponent, deserve much of the blame for humanity's failure to realize their godhood.

It's strange, then, that in spite of this antagonism toward orthodox Christianity, many New Age proponents claim to be Christians. Marianne Williamson, author of the bestsellers *A Return to Love* and *A Woman's Worth*, says that she is a Christian but then goes on to say that "With an enlightened view of Christmas, we understand that it is within our power, through God, to give birth to a divine Self. With an enlightened view of Easter, we understand that this Self is the power of the universe, before which death itself has no real power."[38] In other words, she holds to the traditional New Age belief that she is god.

M. Scott Peck, author of the bestseller *The Road Less Travelled*, also claims to be a Christian. His definition of a Christian, however, has nothing to do with Christianity and provides us with a clue about the New Age attitude toward religions in general:

> To define a 'true Christian' is a risky business.
> But if I had to, my definition would be that a
> true Christian is anyone who is 'for Jesus a
> pleasant place of shelter.' There are hundreds
> of thousands who go to Christian churches
> every Sunday who are not the least bit willing
> to be displeasing to themselves . . . and who are

not, therefore, for Jesus a pleasant place of shelter. Conversely, there are millions of Hindus, Buddhists, Muslims, Jews, atheists, and agnostics who are willing to bear that trial.[39]

This underscores the New Age belief that there are many paths to God, and that many religions can lead you to Him. In order to be tolerant of Christianity, many New Age adherents re-define Christianity to dispose of Christ's exclusive claim of Lordship. Such a re-definition is not really a problem for people who have rejected absolute truth. Indeed, the New Age worldview tends to focus on experience and feelings, often at the expense of reason. Reason can be useful for the New Age adherent, but it also places limits on thought and feelings, and man should never allow himself to be limited. New Age proponents are quite willing to re-define terms and even all of reality since they, as god, create reality. The incredible vanity that goes along with believing you are god is best articulated by Shirley MacLaine, who describes a discussion she held around her dinner table:

> I began by saying that since I realized I created my own reality in every way, I must therefore admit that, in essence, *I was the only person alive in my universe.* I could feel the instant shock waves undulate around the table. I went on to express my feeling of total responsibility *and power* for all events that occur in the world because the world is happening only in my reality. *And* human beings feeling pain, terror,

depression, panic, and so forth, were really
only aspects of pain, terror, depression, panic,
and so on, in me! If they were all characters in
my reality, my dream, then of course they were
only reflections of myself.

I was beginning to understand what the
great masters had meant when they said 'you
are the universe.' If we each create our own
reality, then of course we are everything that
exists within it.[40]

Pointing out here that the New Age worldview fits with the
Frankenstein crowd is quite an understatement. Not only does
a New Age proponent believe that they are good, they believe
that they are god, and therefore in a sense the only person alive
in the universe. The doctrine of the sinfulness of man is truly
antithetical to everything that the New Age proponent holds
dear.

Man must not be told that he is sinful, but instead reminded that he can trust his feelings and desires. Christianity
should, according to feminist Gloria Steinem, "stop telling us
we are innately sinful, and encourage the godlikeness and self-
authority in each of us instead."[41] Doing that would help men
and women recognize that "Each of us has an inner compass
that helps us know where to go and what to do."[42]

SANTA-ISM

C.S. Lewis, in his classic *The Screwtape Letters*, imagines
how an experienced demon might advise a "junior" demon,
especially with regard to keeping people from following Christ.

At one point the older demon recommends to the younger, "If you can once get [the human you're tempting] to the point of thinking that 'religion is all very well up to a point,' you can feel quite happy about his soul. A moderated religion is as good for us as no religion at all—and more amusing."[43] This wishy-washy, comfortable religion that does not challenge or awe us is best described as Santa-ism.

Never heard of Santa-ism? That's not surprising—I made it up. But it's a useful term, because it describes a worldview that is often ignored today. Santa-ists are simply people who believe in a "safe" god rather than the God of the Bible.

Especially prevalent in America today, Santa-ism relies on the fuzzy belief that some god-like being created us and loves us, and doesn't care at all how we behave as long as we don't hurt each other. This jovial Santa Claus god likes us, and he likes it when we ask him for things. Adherents to this worldview don't worry too much about truth or morality, because the grandfather god wants everyone to spend eternity playing harps with him in heaven. As Christian author William Kilpatrick explains, "The secular mind does not always find it necessary to deny God, but it must always reduce Him to a comfortable size. Above all else He must be a manageable God who does not watch or judge."[44]

In many ways, Santa-ism is an offshoot of deism, which was the worldview of some of America's founding fathers (including Thomas Jefferson and Benjamin Franklin). Deists believe that some mystical "First Cause" set the universe in motion, and then abandoned man. Since man has been left to follow his own devices, he need not fear judgment.

This "god-leaves-us-alone-until-we-pray-when-we-need-a-gift" mentality is necessarily hazy, because it doesn't stand up to close scrutiny. Still, we can begin with the Santa-ist's assumptions about god and logically derive his views about man.

If god is non-judgmental, then it follows that every person's thoughts and actions are good enough to please god. According to this view, we haven't separated ourselves from god at all (there is no original sin), and regardless of what we do, he'll welcome us to heaven with open arms. Santa-ists may take exception with Adolf Hitler or the man who beats his dog, but every other person, they believe, is good enough to be accepted by god into his presence.

Interestingly, Karl Barth categorizes Santa-ists as atheists:

> The atheism that is the real enemy is the 'Christianity' that professes faith in God very much as a matter of course, perhaps with great emphasis, and perhaps with righteous indignation at atheism wild or mild, while in its practical thinking and behaviour it carries on exactly as if there were no God. . . . God is thus turned into an item in the inventory of the contents of an old-fashioned or partially modernized house, a piece of furniture the owner would refuse to part with in any circumstances, but for which he has nevertheless ceased to have any real use; or rather, which he has very good reasons for taking care not to use, for it might be uncomfortable or dangerous.[45]

Santa-ists can be found almost everywhere, even in your church. You may not see them until Christmas or Easter, but when those holidays arrive they stride magnanimously into the sanctuary to take a little dose of religion, sort of like an inoculation. As you welcome these Santa-ists into your church—and you *should* welcome them, with grace and kindness—you should ask yourself: Are they comfortable? Perhaps a little too comfortable?

The words of Christ should drive a man out of his La-Z Boy and right down to his knees. Complacency is the domain of the Frankenstein crowd. The Hyde crowd should feel first a desperate need to be reconciled to God, and then intense gratitude and a fierce desire to please the one Who died to reconcile us.

"I believe it to be a grave mistake," writes Christian author Dorothy Sayers, "to present Christianity as something charming and popular with no offense in it."[46] The Bible charges out of the gate with a message that is grievously offensive to everyone: the horror story that we are terrible sinners, that even our righteous acts are like filthy rags (Isaiah 64:6).

This does not mean that your pastor must preach Jonathan Edwards' "Sinners in the Hands of an Angry God" sermon every Sunday. It means, simply, that Christianity has a radically different view of the nature of man, and people had better understand that view or they will understand nothing else about our faith.

S UCH   A   W ORM   AS   I

Which brings us to a sticky point. We have completed our survey of the ten most influential non-Christian worldviews, so you have met most of the religions derived from the assumption that man is basically good. The non-Christian religions that we haven't discussed, like B'hai or Christian Science, also begin by believing in the monster of Frankenstein. But it must be said here that many people who call themselves Christians, and many people who are Christians, misrepresent doctrine and lean toward Frankenstein more than Hyde.

Tragically, many mainline denominations have decided that sin is a dirty word. In an effort to make Christianity more palatable, many pastors, lay leaders, and self-proclaimed spokesmen for Christ discard the bad news of man's inherent rebelliousness and replace it with some milk-and-water concept like man's lack of self-esteem. Episcopal priest Leo Booth, for example, wrote a book chastising orthodox Christians for thinking that man is completely lost and powerless in his unredeemed state. He calls the desperate clinging to Christ that results from a healthy knowledge of our own sinfulness "religious addiction":

> [Religious addiction is] using God, a Church, or a belief system as an escape from reality, in an attempt to find or elevate a sense of self-worth or well-being. It is using God or religion as a fix. It is the ultimate form of co-dependency—feeling worthless in and of ourselves and looking outside ourselves for something or someone to tell us we are worthwhile.[47]

Another Christian author, Anthony A. Hoekema, is equally appalled at the suggestion that men and women might be dead in their sins. He criticizes the traditional hymn "Alas, and Did My Savior Bleed?" by Isaac Watts because it speaks of "such a worm as I." Hoekema feels that this "hymn could convey to many people a quite unflattering self-image."[48]

One can only imagine how he feels about Christ's response to the rich ruler, "No one is good—except God alone" (Luke 18:19).

Last Christmas eve, I attended a service conducted by a pastor who doesn't like the idea of sin. The sermon was a very trying time for me, made more so when I heard the benediction: we were charged in the name of Christ to "find a cause you can live for" and "a self you can live with." My heart ached as I thought of all the people leaving the service who would never find a self they could live with because they never nailed their old sinful self to the cross with Christ. How intensely frustrating to believe that you're good enough to find your own way, only to stumble in the dark again and again.

Countless worldviews are prepared to tell man that he can save himself; only the Christian worldview asks man to swallow the bitter pill of inherent sinfulness. One of the most misguided things a person can do, then, is to act as though Christianity is just like every other worldview. And yet too many "Frankensteins in Hyde's clothing"—Christians who don't understand doctrine—are willing to do just that, to throw away the bad news and consequently render meaningless the good news in the Bible. If, says Kilpatrick, their "optimism about raw human nature is correct, then Christianity is not necessary: Christ's redemptive action on the cross becomes superfluous. After all, why should He have suffered and died to redeem us if there is nothing wrong with us?"[49]

Christians who downplay man's sinfulness need to be reminded: "Selling sin short is only the reverse side of selling God short."[50]

THE STRANGEST ANIMAL

The problem, of course, is that many people—from atheists to Hindus to inconsistent Christians—want to make our consciences rest a little easier. They have experienced (just as everyone has experienced) the awful feeling of falling into the same gross, sinful pattern that they vowed would never happen again. They know the anguish that comes from missing the mark and realizing that they will probably miss it again tomorrow. And so they seek to simplify things by claiming that we're really not that bad, that we really can rescue ourselves.

To believe this, though, one must take one's eyes off men. The Frankenstein crowd can believe in their monster only so long as they don't look too closely at real human beings, those strange animals who laugh and love and fight and cry. The Christian response should begin with a reminder of how odd man really is.

One such reminder is provided by—surprise—Stevenson. Although his words are colored with evolutionary assumptions, his description of man in *Pulvis et Umbra* rings true:

> [W]e look and behold [man] instead filled
> with imperfect virtues: infinitely childish, often
> admirably valiant, often touchingly kind;
> sitting down, amidst his momentary life, to
> debate of right and wrong and the attributes of
> the deity; rising up to do battle for an egg or
> die for an idea . . . To touch the heart of his
> mystery, we find in him one thought, strange
> to the point of lunacy: the thought of duty; the

thought of something owing to himself, to his
neighbour, to his God: an ideal of decency, to
which he would rise if it were possible; a limit
of shame, below which, if it be possible, he will
not stoop. . . . Of all earth's meteors, here at
least is the most strange and consoling: that
this ennobled lemur, this hair crowned bubble
of the dust, this inheritor of a few years and
sorrows, should yet deny himself his rare
delights, and add to his frequent pains, and live
for an ideal . . .[51]

As strange as it seems, it appears that here too Stevenson agrees
with the Christian sentiment so eloquently described by
Alexander Solzhenitsyn: "[T]he line dividing good and evil
cuts through the heart of every human being."[52] Every unredeemed man knows what is good but fails to do the good.

Viktor Frankl is a brilliant psychotherapist who survived
Auschwitz and all the horrors of Nazi death camps. He saw
human nature at its worst—and yet, in the darkest hour, he
also saw human nature at its best: "After all, man is that being
who has invented the gas chambers of Auschwitz; however, he
is also that being who has entered those gas chambers upright,
with the Lord's Prayer or the *Shema Yisrael* on his lips."[53]

The contradiction is astounding, and it should cause us to
cry out as Blaise Pascal does, "What sort of freak then is man!
How novel, how monstrous, how chaotic, how paradoxical,
how prodigious! Judge of all things, feeble earthworm, reposi-
tory of truth, sink of doubt and error, glory and refuse of the
universe!"[54]

When a man looks deeply in the mirror and then considers

the men around him, he realizes that the Frankenstein view is too simplistic. Men can be both bestial and heroic. To say that man is basically good is to forget the Inquisition and belittle the martyrs. Even children can recognize this, according to psychologist Bruno Bettelheim:

> There is a widespread refusal to let children know that the source of much that goes wrong in life is due to our very own natures—the propensity of all men for acting aggressively, asocially, selfishly, out of anger and anxiety. Instead, we want our children to believe that, inherently, all men are good. But children know that *they* are not always good; and often, even when they are, they would prefer not to be. This contradicts what they are told by their parents and therefore makes the child a monster in his own eyes.[55]

Believe in the monster of Frankenstein, and you will become a monster in your own eyes. Believe in the monster of Hyde, and you may, by the grace of God, see your monster slain and replaced by a saint.

"Certainly nothing jolts us more rudely than this doctrine [inherent sinfulness], and yet, but for this mystery, the most incomprehensible of all, we remain incomprehensible to ourselves,"[56] writes Pascal.

To understand ourselves and other men, we must understand one of the central differences between Christianity and every other worldview: "No religion," says Pascal, "except our own has taught that man is born sinful, no philosophical sect has said so, so none has told the truth."[57] It is this truth which allows us to look at the heights of others' heroism and the depths of our own depravity and still have hope.

"We tend to forget," writes Kilpatrick, "how very different a thing Christianity is—how decisively and uncomfortably different."[58] But the great Christian apologists don't forget; they understand that it is precisely where Christianity breaks with all other worldviews that we find Christianity proclaiming its good news the loudest.

The good news starts with the bad. Chesterton tells a mystery story about a judge who is growing tired of all the sin and suffering that parades before his bench. Early in the story, the judge is confronted by the Prime Minister of England, and he explodes at this world leader in front of the whole court: "Get a new soul. That thing's not fit for a dog. Get a new soul."[59]

All of us, at some time in our lives, have done something that makes us so ashamed we feel that we need a new soul. The Frankenstein crowd responds by telling us that these feelings are untrue—that we really can make ourselves pure. The Hyde crowd responds by telling us to trust that experience. Indeed, our only hope is to recognize the depths of our sinfulness and cry out for God to graciously provide that new soul.

Fyodor Dostoyevsky, in a semi-autobiographical work, says that "We are stillborn, and for generations past have not been begotten by living fathers . . ."[60] Pascal says that "Unless we know ourselves to be full of pride, ambition, concupiscence, weakness, wretchedness and unrighteousness, we are truly blind."[61]

If these Hyde enthusiasts are right—if the Bible is true—then you are incapable of saving yourself, and you can't be rescued by any other man, club, organization, government, or ideology. As Lewis warns, "[N]ever, never pin your whole faith on any human being: not if he's the best and wisest in the whole world."[62] Kilpatrick agrees: "Christianity says you can't depend on yourself and you can't ultimately depend on others either."[63]

We must instead depend on God, expecting Him to rescue us. Understanding our own predicament allows us to receive God's grace. "To make a man a saint," says Pascal, "grace is certainly needed, and anyone who doubts this does not know what a saint, or a man, really is."[64] Again, "Man is nothing but a subject full of natural error that cannot be eradicated except through grace."[65]

This was driven home to me one fall day as I walked on the beach with a man who had heard me teach. As he explained to me that he didn't yet believe in Christ and asked me questions about my faith, I prayed silently that the Holy Spirit would speak through me and open his eyes. My prayers accelerated as we turned around and began walking home, because at that point I could measure, step by step, how much longer I'd have the opportunity to talk with him. I felt that I was answering his questions to the best of my ability, but I also knew that my ability wasn't going to save anyone, and that you can't argue a person into the kingdom of heaven. People don't get saved by syllogisms.

As we came to the end of the walk and the end of the discussion, my mind was as blank as a broken television, except for one question that I really didn't want to ask: "Do you know you're a sinner?" The question had popped into my brain some time ago, but I steadily ignored it. How could I ask that of someone I barely knew? How could I ask it of anyone? To my ears, the question sounded as brutal as "Do you know you're going to hell?"

But God was gracious and He caused me to ask the question. And He was gracious, too, because this man looked at me and answered, "Yes."

And once you've said "yes," there's not a whole lot left to say. Once you recognize that you're a sinner—understanding that this implies that nothing you do can save you—where can you go to get clean? Neither Buddha nor Mohammed nor Joseph Smith nor Shirley MacLaine can save you if you've separated yourself from God and can't "un-separate" yourself—only Christ's work is sufficient. Once you understand you're a sinner, you understand Who your only hope can be.

That's how it worked on the beach in Oregon. Not by my wisdom or my power—not because "Do you know you're a sinner?" is a magic question that should be used in every witnessing scenario—but simply because God convicted a man of his own sinfulness and his own need for redemption. As soon as you understand the bad news, you are in a position to recognize the good.

The difference between Christianity and every other faith begins with two monsters. Once you understand which monster roams our world, you are prepared to articulate your own beliefs, and to explain some of the problems with other worldviews. You should look eagerly for opportunities to discuss these problems and share your faith. There are, however, several things you and I should *not* do.

SIN AND HUMILITY

I should *not* run out to the mall and start pointing my

finger and yelling "Sinner!" at people. Most folks don't like to be reminded of their sin—especially in public, especially by a stranger. Besides, many moderns are not "religiously literate"—that is, they aren't familiar with religious concepts. The word "sinner" may not mean anything to them, or it may mean something to them that I didn't intend for it to mean.

Even more importantly, I should *not* get haughty. The more a Christian understands his worldview the more it becomes clear that his faith is true and applicable to all of reality—and that's exciting. As we grow in our faith, the little light bulb comes on that says, "Hey, Christ really meant it when He called Himself the Way, the Truth and the Life. Christianity really is true and the rest of the world really is deceived!" And then, unfortunately, a prideful voice whispers, "Aren't I perceptive to see that Christianity is true and that every other worldview is bankrupt? I am one smart monkey." If we listen to this whisper, we allow ourselves to be deceived into thinking that we somehow rescued ourselves by being clever enough to see the truth. Once we buy into this lie, we begin to treat non-Christians condescendingly—how can anyone be stupid enough to believe in the New Age movement, or any other false worldview? And our arrogance, of course, disgusts those who most need to hear about the gift God has given every man.

Not surprisingly, the secret to avoiding this arrogance is to remember what kind of monster you are. If we can really remember what a wretch we were before God graciously rescued us, and if we can really remember how often we still act wretchedly, then we will never believe the absurd lie that we saw clearly enough to save ourselves. *God* saved us! And before He saved us we were every bit as blind as the blindest atheist we know. Christians are not smarter, faster, stronger, or cuter than non-Christians (it may be just the opposite, when you consider Christ's sympathy toward the poor in spirit)—we simply have, by God's grace, been handed the right pair of glasses.

Lewis rightly points out that "the Christian has a great advantage over other men, not by being less fallen than they nor less doomed to live in a fallen world, but by knowing that he *is* a fallen man in a fallen world . . ."[66] As long as we understand that we have this advantage not because we're clever, but simply because God changed our hearts, then we should be able to convey it graciously to others. The Christian's job is *not* to speak the truth! It is to speak the truth *in love* (Ephesians 4:14-15). If we don't remember this last part, we won't really be showing anyone any truth at all.

The rest of this book will deal simply with the implications of accepting or rejecting the Christian view of man. As John Vasconcellos says, the "practical implications can be seen in every sphere of life, for our choices about how we pursue any human relationship always proceed from the fundamental view of human nature that each of us holds. It is essential that we recognize for ourselves and acknowledge to others our particular personal vision."[67] What might surprise you about Mr. Vasconcellos is that he is a card-carrying member of the Frankenstein crowd—in fact, he is the man most responsible for organizing the California Task Force to Promote Self-Esteem (an agency funded by, you guessed it, the taxpayers). It is not just Christians who understand the importance of a person's beliefs about the nature of man; and it is not just Christians who can defend their choice of monsters.

Christians and the world disagree about the nature of man, and both camps cannot be right. What you believe about the nature of man is not just a matter of opinion. Men either are basically good or inherently sinful—they cannot be both. Either Frankenstein or Hyde stalks the earth. If Christians are wrong, then we are hopelessly deluded and we are leading others astray. In this case, men like James J.D. Luce, who believes that "the fundamentalist experience can be a serious mental health hazard to perhaps millions of people"[68] may not be far from the truth. If he is right, the best and wisest thing that the Frankenstein crowd can do is help the deceived and the blind—Christians—to stop believing that they are sinful.

Likewise, if Christians are right about the nature of man, the kindest thing we can do is help others to understand their condition. If Chesterton is right that non-Christians "are walking in their sleep and try to wake themselves up with nightmares,"[69] then it would be far better to wake them up with the truth.

As we examine the implications of joining either monster camp, it will become more and more clear that we must choose wisely. One of the two thieves who died beside Jesus must have been right; and the other must have been hopelessly wrong. "For those two men who actually died alongside my Savior," says Christian ministry leader Charles Colson, "are representative of all mankind. We either recognize our sinful selves, our sentence of death, and our deserving of that sentence, which leads us to repent and believe—or we curse God and die."[70]

Christians' faith in God is predicated on the fact that they know they shouldn't have too much faith in men. The world's faith in men causes them to grow disinterested in faith in God. Only one faith can be reasonable, and true.

"Repeal all compromises—repeal the Declaration of Independence—repeal all past history; you still cannot repeal human nature."[1]
—Abraham Lincoln

CHAPTER 2

BLIND FAITH

As I sat in the back row of the gym listening to the music, I could feel uneasiness envelop me like a fog. Wasn't this supposed to be a Christmas concert?

The fourth and fifth graders certainly were wearing lots of red and green, and it was only a week before Christmas, but the songs they sang gave little indication of the holiday. In fact, as I listened to my nephews and the rest of the public school students slog through their repertoire, it dawned on me that not one of their songs mentioned Jesus, or the wise men, or any other hint that Christmas was a Christian holiday.

You might expect that a program that excludes every traditional Christmas hymn would at least be mercifully short, but in this case you'd be wrong. Though Christian songs were excluded, the students sang a Hanukkah song, a melody celebrating Kwanzaa (an African holiday based on harvest festivals), and a Druidic song about mistletoe! I found myself wondering vaguely if the encore would be an ancient Egyptian sun-worship chant.

And as I walked out of that gym and into the cold winter night, the clear air carried one clear thought into my head: I had just seen everything that is wrong with the modern American version of separation of church and state.

Many people, including some Christians, would defend the content of that Christmas concert based on separation of church and state. After all, the United States Supreme Court has interpreted the first amendment to say that the state cannot endorse any religious view. According to this interpretation, the Christian worldview should not be "promoted" in state schools because it may cause some students to feel that the state sanctions Christianity as the official religion. For this same reason, the Ten Commandments should not be posted on courthouse walls, and nativity scenes should not appear on public land.

Based on this logic, the American Civil Liberties Union has worked tirelessly to eradicate any hint of Christianity from anything touched by the state (and what doesn't fall within the state's jurisdiction today?). Many organizations and cultural leaders have been scrupulous about keeping the specter of Hyde out of the public square—but their diligence turns to indolence when faced with other religions.

Consider our concert again. The organizers discriminately censored every hint of the Christian religion from their program, but they failed miserably at censoring other religions. Christianity was kept out, but Judaism, paganism, and atheism were welcomed with open arms.

Separation of church and state is too often interpreted by too many people as "separation of *Christianity* and state." The Frankenstein crowd is more than happy to hustle Hyde out of the program, but they often look the other way when elements of other religions, like meditation or spontaneous generation, find their way into the classroom. If we are to be fair, this obvious discrimination against Christianity must change.

But it must not change in the way that most non-Christians imagine. The typical non-Christian response to this argument is to acknowledge that some discrimination has taken place and to promise to be more diligent about excluding other religions from government programs. Many secularists admit that programs like this Christmas concert demonstrate bias, and then they vow to remove all bias in the future. This is not what the Christian expects.

The Christian does not expect this because he does not expect the impossible. He does not ask that every hint of religion be removed from government programs because that would require replacing every government employee with a robot.

Every thinking person is religious; every thinking person has a worldview. To imply that religion can be separated from the state is to imply that some people can think, talk and act without reference to their own faith, which is an absurd implication. The way we behave every day is predicated on the way we understand reality, on our beliefs about the way the world works. For example: virtually every public school teacher tells his or her students that cheating is wrong and will be punished. But to teach your students this is to share with them part of your faith—namely, your belief that it is better to earn something than to steal it—and thus to force your religious convictions on the class.

Should the teacher allow students to cheat, rather than imposing his beliefs on them? Of course not. To promote order and justice in the classroom, every teacher must necessarily teach his students to adhere to certain faith-based values.

Or consider Congress. As elected representatives, these men and women are supposed to create laws that represent the will of their electorate. But this mandate does not require them to sacrifice their own consciences; a representative who votes for a bill he believes to be unethical is a coward and a failure. A voter's faith should affect the way he votes, whether he is a private citizen in the voting booth or a senator in D.C. We expect our government officials to act consistently with their professed religion, be it Buddhism, Christianity or any other.

Put simply, we can no more separate religion from the state than we can separate people from their thoughts. No one is neutral—everyone makes certain assumptions about the nature of man and the nature of God, and these assumptions impact the way we behave every day. Blaise Pascal describes the completely neutral man as someone who must doubt everything—even doubting that he is doubting and doubting that he exists. "No one," says Pascal, "can go that far, and I maintain that a perfectly genuine sceptic has never existed."[2] G.K. Chesterton agrees:

> [I]t is stark hypocrisy to pretend that nine-tenths of the higher critics and scientific evolutionists and professors of comparative religion are in the least impartial. Why should they be impartial, what is being impartial, when the whole world is at war about whether one thing [Christianity] is a devouring superstition or a divine hope?[3]

Every thinking person makes faith assumptions. The public school principal who sought to hire only non-religious teachers would never hire even one person, let alone an entire faculty.[4]

Separation of church and state, as it is defined today, is an unattainable ideal. Instead of maintaining an unrealistic policy that ensures hit-and-miss discrimination against religions, the

Supreme Court should take a closer look at the first amendment and the intent of our founding fathers, and focus strictly on avoiding the establishment of any one religion as the official national religion. This realistic approach allows for a proper separation of the Christian church and the state, recognizing the limits on the jurisdiction of both institutions while affording government employees of every faith the opportunity to think and live according to their consciences, without fear of attracting discrimination.[5]

Unfortunately, this isn't likely to happen in the near future. The modern distortion of separation of church and state will continue as long as Americans accept another more foundational myth: the dichotomy between faith and reason.

WORLDVIEWS ARE RELIGIOUS

When most people talk about religions today, they are usually referring to worldviews that profess some belief in God or the supernatural. They then contrast this "blind faith" in things we cannot see (like angels and souls) with reason. Many people today think that faith and reason are two mutually exclusive things—that a person uses *faith* when they don't have any good reasons for thinking something, and *reason* when they have solid evidence for thinking something. But this contrast between faith and reason distorts both terms and results in absurd conclusions, like the expectation that Christians will think like Christians only within the four walls of the church.

No one disputes that Christians have faith, as do New Age proponents, Mormons, Jews, Muslims, etc. Everyone understands these worldviews to be religious, but many people would claim that Marxism or other forms of atheism are *not* religious and do not require faith. Christians like Charles J. McFadden, however, disagree: "We must be made to understand that Communism is *not* a mere political, military, and economic movement. . . . Communism is basically a philosophy of life—*a false religion.*"⁶

As was noted in chapter one, every thinking person assumes certain things—on faith—about God and man. These core beliefs form the foundation for every worldview, from atheism to Christianity. Whether or not a person believes in God or the supernatural, that person still exercises faith to create his framework for understanding existence. *Every* worldview begins with faith; therefore every worldview is religious.⁷

Another way to look at this is to remember a word that non-Christians love to use to label Christians: *dogmatic.* This word implies that Christians have doctrine—basic beliefs— upon which they cannot compromise. An orthodox Christian must believe in the historical Resurrection, for example, and if he ceases to believe in the Resurrection, he ceases to be orthodox.

Secularists imply that this dogmatism causes Christians to be narrow-minded and intolerant, whereas other worldviews, because they are not dogmatic, are open-minded and tolerant. But a moment's reflection will remind you that every thinking person is dogmatic.

Do you believe in the New Age worldview? Then you hold to certain doctrines upon which you are not willing to compromise. Shirley MacLaine articulates the most sacrosanct New Age belief: "What is the center of the universe? Every place is the center. Who is the center? *Everyone* is the center.

Where is God? God, and the energy from which all has been created, is in everything . . ."[8] New Age proponents cling dogmatically to pantheism, as well as to spiritual evolution, reincarnation, and the belief that all is one. They are not "open-minded" about the possibility that man is inherently sinful, for example, because they have already accepted the doctrine that man is god.

This holds true with all other religions that profess belief in the supernatural. Buddhists assert dogmatically that suffering should be avoided; traditional Jews proclaim that they are God's chosen people; Hindus believe dogmatically that your karma dictates your next incarnation; Christian Scientists will not compromise on their belief that God can heal you if you have enough faith; Muslims are emphatic that only one God exists; Jehovah's Witnesses are committed to the belief that Jesus was a created being; and even Santa-ists believe dogmatically that God will not judge their actions too harshly.

This also holds true for atheistic worldviews. Although atheists like to claim that they are not religious and have no dogma, these claims are unrealistic. Atheists begin, like everyone, with a faith assumption that must be true in order for their worldview to be true. In their case, they assume that only the physical world exists—that there is no such thing as the supernatural. The signatories of the *Humanist Manifesto II* state this faith in dogmatic terms: "Nature may indeed be broader and deeper than we know; any new discoveries, however, will but enlarge our knowledge of the natural."[9]

Such a claim requires a great deal of faith: the atheist must trust that not only God, but also angels, demons, Satan, heaven, hell, and the soul do not exist. How do atheists know that these things do not exist? Typically, an atheist responds by asserting that he has never seen, touched, tasted, heard or smelled these objects—that is, he has no empirical evidence for their existence—and so they cannot exist. The atheist equates empiricism with reality, and concludes that he has used pure reason to deduct that only the natural world exists.

Christians would do well to remind the atheist of another monster story here. In *Dracula*, the two protagonists wrestle with a rash of deaths marked by no more serious symptom than small puncture wounds on the neck. Dr. John Seward, a scientist who will only believe in things he can see, cannot imagine what caused these deaths. His comrade gently reminds him that there still might be a supernatural explanation, chastising him as the Christian worldview chastises the atheist: "Ah, it is the fault of our science that it wants to explain all; and if it explain not, then it says there is nothing to explain."[10]

The atheist's faith in science or empiricism as the only way to know is precisely that, *faith*. Supernatural things generally do not manifest themselves physically—they are, by definition, "super-" (beyond) nature. To dismiss the supernatural because you've never seen it is analogous to the color-blind man dismissing the color red because he's never seen it. Christians respond to this assertion by noting that we would generally expect things that are not physical not to manifest themselves in physical ways.

The atheist dogmatically ignores this response and all other assertions about the existence of the supernatural, believing faithfully that everyone who claims to have experienced the supernatural is deceived. Ever since Adam, countless men and women have testified that they have seen, touched, and even wrestled with supernatural beings. Atheists must ignore what Chesterton calls this "choking cataract of human testimony in favor of the supernatural."[11] The atheist must, on faith, reject this cataract of experiences as myths, illusions, and lies.

Right out of the gate, then, the atheist shows himself to be more dogmatic than any Christian. "The believers in miracles accept them (rightly or wrongly) because they have evidence for them," says Chesterton. "The disbelievers in miracles deny them (rightly or wrongly) because they have a doctrine against them."[12] Open-minded? Hardly. Talk to an atheist about God, and you will find yourself talking to a closed, barred, locked and double-locked mind.[13]

BEYOND FREEDOM AND DIGNITY

Which brings us to B.F. Skinner. All atheists are dogmatic, but it is difficult to find any more consistently dogmatic than Skinner. This 20th century psychologist popularized *behaviorism,* a school of thought which asserts that, since only the physical world exists, man must be understood as a physical machine that behaves the way his physical environment programs him to behave. Although some atheists are repelled by the implications of behaviorism, it bears discussion because it is logically consistent with atheism, and because it introduces more doctrines that require great faith to accept.

The reason some atheists reject behaviorism will become clear momentarily; for now, it is enough to recognize that some do, and that this rejection is not based on logic. The consistent atheist must embrace behaviorism, but many atheists would rather sacrifice their intellectual integrity than face the conclusions demanded by their worldview.

Although every atheist will deny the existence of God, angels, demons, Satan, heaven, hell, and souls, many balk at the other supernatural concepts that Skinner and his theory happily jettison, and it is here that behaviorists and less consistent atheists part ways.

Not only does Skinner discard all the aforementioned supernatural concepts, but he also denies the existence of thought, mind, freedom and dignity. His book *Beyond Freedom and Dignity* is not metaphorical; he means quite simply that man must move beyond concepts like freedom and dignity because they simply are not real.[14]

Skinner's logic is fiendishly simple: beginning with the faith assumption that only the natural world exists, he concludes logically enough that concepts like mind and thought are inappropriate—that only the brain exists, and our "thoughts" are only chemical synapses firing in our brain. No neurosurgeon has ever cut open a patient and dissected a thought, but most neurosurgeons are quite familiar with the plain physical processes of the brain. These processes, according to Skinner, account for all that we believe to be our mind and thoughts. "[M]ind," he says, "is a myth, with all the power of myths."[15]

Understanding that soul and mind are myths requires Skinner to conclude that purely physical stimuli are responsible for motivating our brain and causing us to "think" and act. Man, in other words, is just a bundle of stimuli receptors waiting for his environment (the food he eats, the weather, sounds, etc.) to determine what he does next. Man *behaves* in response to the stimuli he receives. To understand this concept, it might be helpful to remember the experiments of another behaviorist, Ivan Pavlov. In his famous experiment with dogs, he demonstrated that a dog can be stimulated to salivate by ringing a bell, even when food is not present. The behaviorist believes that man's behavior is, in the same way, determined by his physical environment.

Clearly, if this is the case, man does not have free will. Concepts like *choice* and *responsibility* are meaningless; man does not choose, but rather is dictated to by the world around him. If you find yourself reading this book, you are doing so not because you wanted to but because the humidity is 32%, your body temperature is 98.7 degrees, you had cold pizza for breakfast, your parents spanked you when you were three . . . and so on. You get the idea.

According to this view, if you ever find yourself doing something really rotten, like knocking off a liquor store, don't feel bad. You did not choose to commit the crime, but rather you were determined by your environment to behave that way. The police shouldn't hold you responsible—society made you do it (which monster does this sound like?).

If you have a habit of knocking off liquor stores, this might sound like a pretty good theory. It allows you to behave however you please, and then blames your environment for your behavior. Your whole life is not your responsibility—you needn't take any blame.

But you also can't take any credit. No choice you made, no matter how base *but also* no matter how noble or dignified, was really a choice. Just as you were forced to knock off the liquor store, you were also forced to dive in front of the bus to rescue the child. You shouldn't receive any medals or rewards—even any pats on the back—because saving that child was the action determined by your physical environment. You could have chosen no other way—at that moment in time, or at any other moment in your life. No action, no attitude, and nothing you become are ever a result of your choosing. At the end of your life, even if you lived as properly as one of the apostles, you could not look back with any pride or sense of accomplishment. As Skinner so aptly noted at the end of his life: "If I am right about human behavior, I have written the autobiography of a nonperson."[16]

It is this side of the coin that should make behaviorism really disturbing to everyone. Have you ever chosen the higher, harder path? Have you ever been noble or wise or perseverant? Not according to behaviorism. Once you throw out free will, you also throw out responsibility—for both your bad actions and your good. Without freedom, man cannot have dignity either. You are a "nonperson," an automaton—you are, as Skinner says, "only the way in which a species and a culture produce more of a species and a culture."[17]

Skinner believed in this theory as fervently as any martyr. His faith that he was right about the non-existence of thought, mind, freedom and dignity drove him to seek to convince others that he was right,[18] and to apply his worldview in practice.

The most chilling example of this practical application is the invention that Skinner called the *heir-conditioner*. Reasoning that negative environmental stimuli are what cause people to behave badly, Skinner sought to protect people from these stimuli as soon as they were born. The way to accomplish this? Put infants in giant glass boxes, called heir-conditioners, and try to keep the child in there as much as possible. In a move stranger than any "Ripley's Believe it or Not," Skinner actually marketed these giant aquariums, hoping that normal families would see the wisdom of keeping their babies in boxes!

By most accounts, Skinner sold only about 1,000 heir-conditioners, but he believed in his invention sufficiently to keep his own daughter, Deborah, in one for much of her first two-and-a-half years. Thankfully, Deborah claims today that her father's misguided faith in his theories had no ill effect on her development.

Skinner, of course, would be shocked to hear his invention and his theories referred to in terms of faith. His decision to put his daughter in a box was, he believed, based on science and reason, not faith. He described himself as applying "scientific method to the study of human behavior."[19]

We have spent so much time dissecting Skinner, however, because his life oozes faith. He was as dogmatic as any Christian about his beliefs. How did Skinner know that the scientific method was a trustworthy means of obtaining knowledge? On faith. How did he know that God, angels, demons, Satan, heaven, hell, souls, mind, thoughts, freedom and dignity did not exist? On faith. How did he know that "there is no reason why progress toward a world in which people may be automatically good should be impeded"?[20] On faith. How did he know that his daughter would benefit more from time in a box than from normal nurturing? On faith. How did he know that nobody really chooses and therefore every individual is a "nonperson"? On faith.

Skinner may have been more dogmatic than most atheists, but only because he was more aware of the logical conclusions demanded by his atheism. Those atheists who reject behaviorism still have faith, but they add to that faith the irrational hope that they can ignore their beliefs when they become inconvenient or don't seem to match reality.

Even setting aside Skinner's particularly unnerving dogmatism, atheists must believe uncompromisingly in, at the very least, all of the following: the non-existence of the supernatural, the general trustworthiness of the five senses, order arising from chaos, history as meaningless,[21] evolution, and spontaneous generation (the hypothesis that life arose from non-life, which would explain the existence of life without reference to a Creator). It's especially noteworthy that atheists should cling dogmatically to these last two doctrines, because both require faith that could move mountains. The Dean of Harvard's biology department (the equivalent of the high priest of evolution), Stephen Jay Gould, admits "the awesome improbability of human evolution."[22] This improbability begins, of course, with spontaneous generation, an event in itself so improbable that scientists for more than a century have tried to create life from non-life and have unanimously failed. Though some of the most intelligent men in the world have dedicated their careers to creating the spark of life from dead matter, no one has ever seen life arise from non-life! How much more difficult to believe, then, that spontaneous generation could occur without the aid of intelligence, billions of years ago strictly as a result of chaotic events.

"[O]ne of the curious things," says William Kilpatrick, "about a secularized society is this: the less it believes in God, the more it believes in miracles."[23]

Though the atheist claims to be unhindered by faith, his claim rings hollow the moment that we consider his unwavering commitment to evolution and spontaneous generation—*events that neither he nor any other human being have ever witnessed.*[24] The atheist, we find, believes "not on what is seen, but on what is unseen" (2 Corinthians 4:18) just as much as the Christian does.

Christians, of course, have been saying this all along. Chesterton makes one of his characters respond to atheistic evolution by exclaiming, "What I complain of is a vague popular philosophy which supposes itself to be scientific when it is really nothing but a sort of new religion and an uncommonly nasty one."[25] Karl Barth argues that "There are also religions disguised in the form of science . . . concealed behind a very demonstrative secularity, which represent superstructures or leaps that are the more vigorous for that very reason, leaps into some sort of beyond, worship of the most diverse gods and idols."[26]

FAITH VS. REASON

Atheists and other proponents of separation of church and state have begun with the assumption that certain worldviews are based completely on reason, and that others are based on a faith that is separate from reason. They then conclude that it is possible to run a government and do science in a religious vacuum. As we have seen, however, every worldview is religious, and therefore every person teaches, performs experiments, and draws conclusions based on faith. Separation of church and state has not removed religions from governmental affairs; it has simply replaced theistic religions with atheistic ones. As Phillip Johnson aptly explains,

> Many people would say that we [in America] have progressed from a de facto religious establishment to a position of neutrality toward religion, but, as I have said, that would be a superficial and misleading way of describing the contemporary situation. What has really happened is that a new established religious

philosophy has replaced the old one. Like the
old philosophy, the new one is tolerant only up
to a point, specifically the point where its own
right to rule the public square is threatened.[27]

In other words, atheists allow theistic people to influence
spheres that are traditionally understood as religious, like the
church and Bible studies, but they quickly grow intolerant
when their own dogma is challenged in the classroom or any
other supposed "secular" arena.

This intolerance, sanctioned by the doctrine of separation
of church and state, has resulted in a state of affairs that sounds
a little like the way things worked in the former Soviet Union.
According to Barbara von der Heydt, the church in the Soviet
Union "was only allowed to hold worship services; nearly all
other overt manifestations of faith were not permitted. Public
discussion of Christianity, Christian education of children, and
all charitable activities were forbidden."[28] America, fortunately,
hasn't progressed this far, but the groundwork has been laid.
By accepting the false dichotomy between faith and reason,
Americans have marginalized Christianity and all other theistic
religions, allowing anyone on the side of "reason" to dismiss
assertions by those on the side of "faith." "Those who try to
challenge naturalism," says Johnson,

> are confined not in a prison cell but in a
> stereotype, and the terms in which the media
> and the textbooks report any controversy are
> defined in a manner designed to prevent
> dangerous ideas from getting serious consider-
> ation. Whatever the critics of naturalism say is

> mere 'religious belief,' in opposition to 'scien-
> tific knowledge'; hence it is, by definition,
> fantasy as opposed to solid fact.[29]

This dichotomy between "fantasy" and "fact"—between "faith" and "reason"—exists only in the mind of secularists, not in reality. Every thinking person bases their life on faith. The Christian and other theists confess their reliance on faith; now it's time for the atheist to spend a little time in confession.

When atheists confess their beliefs, we can begin to discuss the real relationship between faith and reason. Faith and reason aren't opposites like "irrational wishing" and "sound thinking"; rather, they are teammates, working together to help a person arrive at his or her worldview. Since we start out knowing nothing, we've got to make some faith assumptions before we can know anything. Then we can use reason to build a solid structure on those assumptions. If those assumptions are correct and our logic is sound, then our worldview will match reality.

The question is not, Who uses faith and who uses reason? Everyone uses both. The question instead should be, Who has the *most reasonable* faith? Do the faith assumptions you've made provide a firm foundation for your logic, so that your conclusions match your experience and the way in which the world works? If not, there's something wrong with either your faith or your reason, and you're not going to understand reality until you get them fixed.

Is Christianity the most reasonable faith? For many Christians who have been inundated with the "faith vs. reason" lie, it's hard to even think of Christianity as something coherent, something that requires thought as well as emotion. But until Christians think this way, non-Christians will continue to treat our worldview as "blind faith." Until we can articulate the differences between Christianity and other worldviews, and demonstrate that our worldview matches reality better, non-Christians will have very little reason to listen to us in the public square.

True Christianity, according to Pascal, requires two things: "submission and use of reason."[30] How odd, then, that many non-Christians today seem to think Christianity requires gullibility and a blindfold. Christians are largely responsible for this misunderstanding, and as people concerned about our neighbors (and good stewards of our brains), we ought to clear it up.

IS IT REASONABLE TO BELIEVE MEN ARE SINFUL?

A good place to begin this work is with monsters. Non-Christians often wax eloquent about their faith in man, in his goodness and in his progress toward paradise. Sometimes these faith claims are really extravagant. Skinner wrote a novel, *Walden Two*, in which he imagined a community based on the principles of behaviorism. The founder of the community, Frazier, often speaks for Skinner as he describes man's great potential and the hope for the future. At one point Frazier exults, "The one fact that I would cry from every housetop is this: the Good Life is waiting for us—here and now! . . . It doesn't wait upon an improvement in human nature. At this very moment we have the necessary techniques, both material and psychological, to create a full and satisfying life for everyone."[31] H.G. Wells, another atheist author, also wrote a novel in which the protagonist often speaks for him; in *The Time Machine* he makes the hero predict that

> Some day all this will be better organized, and still better. That is the drift of the current in spite of the eddies. The whole world will be intelligent, educated, and co-operating; things will move faster and faster towards the subjugation of Nature. In the end, wisely and carefully we shall readjust the balance of animal and vegetable life to suit our human needs.[32]

This faith that man is good enough and that everything will work out in the end is central to every non-Christian worldview. It is, in some ways, a comforting thing to believe. But is it reasonable? As Dorothy Sayers says, "It is unpleasant to be called sinners, and much nicer to think that we all have hearts of gold—but have we? . . . It is encouraging to feel that progress is making us automatically every day and in every way better, and better, and better—but does history support that view?"[33]

A good question. And fortunately, we live in a world that surrounds us with the answers. Many non-Christians may claim that we can know nothing about God, or heaven, or anything supernatural. They may even balk at philosophical discussions that seem to apply only in the ivory tower. But certainly everyone can agree that it is possible to study man, and to draw some conclusions. Every day we see both the attitude of our own hearts and the actions of other men. Do these attitudes and actions support the beliefs of the Frankenstein crowd or the Hyde crowd?

Consider man's history: slavery, child labor, the Roman gladiators, gang violence, King Herod, the Crusades, Tiananmen Square, the Spanish Inquisition, barbarian invasion and rape, Auschwitz, abortion, Nero, Joseph Stalin, forced sterilization, Hiroshima, the gulags, treason, Civil War, euthanasia, and cannibalism.

Consider my history: hatred, drunkenness, envy, lust, greed, selfishness, lies, rage, sloth, injustice, and worse things I've thought but never done.

Consider your history.

And then marvel at the fact that people deny the sinfulness of man. "Original sin," says Chesterton, "is the only part of Christian theology which can really be proved."[34] For those people who claim to trust only facts and not faith, sin is a fact as obvious as the heart in their chest:

> Modern masters of science are much impressed
> with the need of beginning all inquiry with a fact.
> The ancient masters of religion were quite equally
> impressed with that necessity. They began with
> the fact of sin—a fact as practical as potatoes.
> Whether or no man could be washed in miracu-
> lous waters, there was no doubt at any rate that
> he wanted washing.[35]

This fact has been treated as self-evident by people throughout history. Abraham Lincoln, in his typical wry fashion, exclaims, "The Bible says somewhere that we are desperately selfish. I think we would have discovered that fact without the Bible."[36] Christian theologian R.C. Sproul agrees: "If the Bible never mentioned original sin, we could easily postulate it from a study of history and human society."[37]

Sin is certainly obvious, though it's also obvious that man is very reluctant to admit his sinfulness. Much of mankind has chosen to ignore the evidence for their sinfulness, because facing one's deficiencies drives one to face the God of the Bible. But if we are honest, says Pascal, we must do exactly that:

> When I see the blind and wretched state of man, when I survey the whole universe in its dumbness and man left to himself with no light, as though lost in this corner of the universe, without knowing who put him there, what he has come to do, what will become of him when he dies, incapable of knowing anything, I am moved to terror, like a man transported in his sleep to some terrifying desert island, who wakes up quite lost and with no means of escape. Then I marvel that so wretched a state does not drive people to despair. I see other people around me, made like myself. I ask them if they are any better informed than I, and they say they are not. Then these lost and wretched creatures look around and find some attractive objects to which they become addicted and attached. For my part I have never been able to form such attachments, and considering how very likely it is that there exists something besides what I can see, I have tried to find out whether God has left any traces of himself.[38]

Who has the most reasonable faith? It would seem, from even a cursory study of man, that the Christian worldview is most reasonable. Pascal's response is a rational response to the morass of sinfulness that threatens to suffocate humanity. It does not take a blind leap of faith to believe that man is inherently sinful and therefore needs a Savior. The evidence in the mirror and in the history books cries out for such a conclusion.

And yet almost every person who is not a Christian chooses to close their eyes when Hyde appears, and make a leap of faith that Frankenstein really exists.

BLAME IT ON SOCIETY

In fairness to non-Christians, however, it should be pointed out that they generally do not deny the existence of evil in the world. Most non-Christians will readily admit that there are very few perfect people—that most folks do bad things occasionally. But they stop short of holding people completely accountable for their actions. Like the monster of Frankenstein, they blame society and the physical environment for their "mistakes." The reason we see bad things happening in the world, they say, is because man finds himself in an imperfect setting—either the government doesn't have enough power, or teachers provide the wrong education, or the church teaches them bad doctrine, or the economic system is oppressive, or suffering deceives them, or they have their authority limited, or temptations lead them astray, or—you name it. Abraham Maslow, a Humanist psychologist, puts it rather bluntly: "Sick people are made by a sick culture; healthy people are made possible by a healthy culture."[39]

On the surface, this seems like an acceptable explanation, but it has at least two problems. First, those who believe in the inherent goodness of man must explain how basically good men can create a "sick culture." After all, isn't society just made up of individuals? If individuals are basically good, from whence does the bad society arise? If, as Mormons believe, we are "gods in embryo," then how do gods have the capacity to create a society filled with temptations and evil? If, as atheists believe, we are evolving toward utopia, why didn't the very first humans (who were also basically good) just make their first society a perfect society?

Second, according to the Frankenstein crowd, we would expect children to be the most perfect people. Youngsters have spent the least amount of time on earth and therefore should be the least tainted by society. But children prove to be every bit as sinful as adults, as Kilpatrick points out:

> So if you want to see what the real self is like,
> you must find people who haven't been twisted
> by society—young children, for instance. Now
> this, it must be admitted, is good advice. If
> you take it, the first thing you discover is that
> the humanists [and other non-Christians]
> haven't looked very closely at children: they are
> not as a rule a good advertisement for the
> natural state.[40]

And again, "The business of snatching toys, refusing to share, hitting little sisters, and lying outrageously to cover it all up begins early enough in the child's life to suggest that the fatal flaw lies not in his society but in his nature."[41]

Interestingly, Maslow recognized this problem, and seemed to change his mind about his theories near the end of his life. After watching his daughters grow up, he noted that his parenting experience "made the psychology of the time look trivial and totally inadequate."[42] He eventually concluded that children could not be "self-actualized" (the term he used to describe people in touch with their basic goodness) because they have not

> learned how to be patient; nor have they
> learned enough about evil in themselves and
> others . . . nor have they generally become
> knowledgeable and educated enough to open
> the possibility of becoming wise; nor have they
> generally acquired enough courage to be
> unpopular, to be unashamed about being
> openly virtuous, etc.[43]

How strange, then, that the Frankenstein crowd's basic faith expects children to be the most patient, wise, courageous, and virtuous!

Yet in spite of all the evidence suggesting that Hyde stalks the earth, the non-Christian's optimism continues, unchanged by time or experience. This optimism loomed large at the beginning of the 20th century, and it looms large today.

FAITH IN MAN

More than a century ago, it looked as though technology could solve every problem, and many people concluded that technology's bounty would cause men to behave better. Once everyone owned a car, or a spaceship, and had little pills that provided all their nutrition in one easy gulp—then man could get on with the business of being good. On January 1, 1900, the *New York World* predicted that the 20th century would "meet and overcome all perils and prove to be the best that this steadily improving planet has ever seen."

If one avoided looking too closely at men, one could find reasons for such optimism. American slavery had finally been abolished, and people were beginning to understand the evils inherent in child labor. The world, it seemed, was growing more merciful—more willing to protect those unable to speak for themselves. And no one could deny that science was improving people's lives. Thanks largely to Louis Pasteur's pioneering work with sterilization, hospitals had ceased to be bacteria-havens. Machines were making it possible for men to produce more without working as hard. You could actually pick up a device and hear your mother 600 miles away in Toledo, gossiping about your hometown! It seemed obvious that man was gaining control of his environment, and could now lend a hand to speed his evolution along.

But the 20th century quickly spun out of control. First men fought the "war to end all wars," and then they fought another. Hitler and his minions treated humans like cattle, exterminating the "unfit" and breeding only the fit. Americans looked the other way (or worse yet, applauded) as Joseph Stalin did much the same thing in the Soviet Union. And then man fought a few more wars. The 20th century turned into the bloodiest century in the history of man, even without factoring in the slaughter caused by legalized abortion and the infanticide perpetuated by China's one-child-per-family policy.

Incredibly, in spite of the ugly turns of the 20th century,

the Frankenstein crowd remains unswerving in their faith. The boldest actually try to interpret the horrible events of the past 100 years as proof that the Christian worldview is wrong, asserting that Christianity cannot account for the existence of evil. But evil is much easier to account for if it exists in the heart of every man than it is if man is good enough to save himself, as Chesterton reminds us: "As for the general view that the Church was discredited by the War—they might as well say that the Ark was discredited by the Flood. When the world goes wrong, it proves rather that the Church is right. The Church is justified, not because her children do not sin, but because they do."[44]

Chesterton's observation falls on deaf ears, however, and so we find much of mankind undaunted by 20th century events, eagerly anticipating the 21st century. Whereas atheists tended to lead the optimistic charge into the 20th century, New Age proponents are on the vanguard today. Some New Age leaders predicted that the moment we entered the new millennium we would experience a leap of consciousness that would initiate a peaceful era known as the "Age of Aquarius." Other New Age leaders are more vague, promising only that man will continue to evolve spiritually until life becomes perfect. Robert Muller, former assistant secretary-general for the United Nations, describes this move toward perfection as a sort of new creation, with man as the creator:

> And God saw that all nations of the earth,
> black and white, poor and rich, from North
> and South, from East and West, and of all
> creeds were sending their emissaries to a tall
> glass house [the United Nations building] on

the shores of the River of the Rising Sun, on
the island of Manhattan, to study together, to
think together and to care together for the
world and all its people. And God said: That is
good. And it was the first day of the New Age
of the earth.[45]

Muller goes on to describe the next five days of this "New
Age," during which men rescue the world from pollution and
exploitation, destroy their weapons and generally create paradise. And on the seventh day, according to Muller, the Lord

looked down upon the earth and said: And
now, my children, you will know again that
each of you is a miracle, a unique creation in
the universe, that life is a sacred gift which you
must cherish at all times, that you were engen-
dered in my image, that happiness and paradise
can be established on earth, that your beautiful, miraculous planet will still spin for eons of
time in the fathomless universe, that you are its
caretakers and keepers, and that when finally
its end comes, every atom of it will be reborn
in another star in heaven. And there shall be
no end to birth, life, death and resurrection in
the eternal stream of the universe which you
will never understand, for this will remain
forever the difference between you and Me. I
will now make My peace with you and let you
establish a perfect Earth. Farewell, My
grownup children. At long last, you are on the

right path, you have brought heaven down to earth and found your proper place in the universe. I will now leave you for a long journey, for I have to turn My sight to other troubled and unfinished celestial bodies. I now pronounce you Planet of God. Be happy. Enjoy fully your divine lives on your miraculous planet with all the care, passion, ecstasy, enthusiasm and love they deserve.[46]

On faith, the Frankenstein crowd sweeps all the horrors and bloodshed of the 20th century (and of all the centuries before) under the rug, and expects better luck next time. Trusting in their own abilities, they expect that their future will look wildly better than the past or the present ever have. Those who refuse to learn from history are, as the cliché goes, doomed to repeat it—and they are also bound to be disappointed.

THE PHILOSOPHER WHO CHANGED HIS MIND

If man is truly sinful, as Christians maintain, then expecting man to be able to make things better is a lot like fighting Muhammad Ali: no matter how many times you get back up, you're going to get knocked down again. "The people who are most discouraged and made despondent by the barbarity and stupidity of human behavior," says Sayers, "are those who think highly of *homo sapiens* . . . and who still cling to an optimistic belief in the civilizing influence of progress and enlightenment."[47] C.E.M. Joad, a 20th century philosopher who spent most of his life as an atheist, agrees:

It is because we rejected the doctrine of original sin that we on the Left were always being disappointed; disappointed by the refusal of people to be reasonable, by the subservience of intellect to emotion, by the failure of true Socialism to arrive, by the behaviour of nations and politicians, by the masses' preference for Hollywood to Shakespeare and for Mr. Sinatra to Beethoven; above all, by the recurrent fact of war.[48]

Such disappointment can, however, lead to overwhelming joy. By God's grace, non-Christians jolted by the disappointment of man's repeated failings can trade in their blind faith for the biblical view of the nature of man. Though the news from the Garden of Eden is very bad indeed, it indicates man's profound need for a Savior—a Savior who is not merely a man but also God. Since only one Savior fits that bill, the man who joins the Hyde crowd finds himself trusting Christ to wash away his sins.

Which is precisely what happened to Joad. For most of his life, Joad loudly proclaimed his distaste for God and the supernatural. He occasionally accompanied Bertrand Russell (a philosopher who made it rather plain how he felt when he wrote *Why I am not a Christian*) on the British Broadcasting Channel to discuss all the flaws and deceit contained in Christianity. By his own admission, Joad "hero-worshipped" George Bernard Shaw (another atheist) and it was thanks to Shaw's influence, says Joad, "that I had become a Socialist, and his most lightly conceived doctrines had for me the authority of gospel. One was precisely this doctrine that evil was due to the external circumstances of men's lives and, in particular, to the circumstance of poverty."[49]

As an atheist, Joad whole-heartedly embraced this belief that man is basically good, and relied on this assumption as good evidence for the necessity of socialism. Even as he survived World War I and World War II, Joad clung to his faith in man's goodness. But the events of the 20th century finally wore down Joad's optimism. As he watched men in his century make the same discouraging choices and commit the same discouraging crimes again and again, he was forced to conclude that his faith in man was "a shallow-rooted plant which, growing to maturity amid the lush and leisured optimism of the nineteenth century, was quite unfitted to withstand the bleaker winds that blow through ours."[50] He considered that the Frankenstein crowd's faith "had been rendered utterly unplausible by the events of the last forty years [1914-1954]."[51]

Joad eventually wrote a book entitled *The Recovery of Belief* which documented his transfer of allegiance from Frankenstein to Hyde. As he rightly understood, this transfer of allegiance also required him to replace his faith in man with faith in Christ. His "new way of looking at things" caused him to search for a Savior and to find One at the foot of the cross. As he says, "[T]his new way of looking at things was only a very old way; was, in fact, the way which I had been taught in my childhood, namely, the Christian way."[52]

As Christians have been saying all along, and as Joad came to understand, his "changed view of the nature of man . . . led to a changed view of the nature of the world."[53] What we believe about man lays the foundation for our entire worldview.

Our belief about man can either conform to the evidence we find in the world around us, or it can flaunt that evidence. Joad exercised blind faith in the goodness of man even as Hitler slaughtered the Jews, but he eventually lost the will to muster that much faith. More accurately, Joad was healed, as Chesterton makes one of his characters say, from the "one spiritual disease," which is "thinking one is quite well."[54] His unreasonable faith in mankind was replaced with the very reasonable faith in the One Who never sinned.

FAITH IN CHRIST

The happy ending to Joad's story underscores the problem with treating faith and reason as opposites. Too many people tend to paint Christianity as an unreasonable faith and other worldviews as pure reason; when in fact, the Christian starts with the very reasonable belief that he can trust the evidence that he finds all around him (and even within him), while non-Christians willfully close their eyes to this evidence and trust blindly that man really can save himself. Incredibly, the present interpretation of the separation of church and state requires the exclusion of the Christian faith from the classroom and much of the public square, and yet welcomes the irrational faith inherent in many non-Christian worldviews. Such discrimination is unjust and (ironically) irrational.

None of which means that only logical people are Christians, or that Christianity requires no faith. The Bible makes it clear that men are saved by grace through faith—not by their own great reasoning powers or by someone else's dazzling logic. Just because Christianity seems so reasonable, we should not expect that all reasonable people will accept it. Many irrational people are Christians, and many brilliant logicians are not.

I've yammered so long about the fact that Christianity is rational not because I think I can make every reasonable person admit that it's true, but because I want to dispel the tired myth that Christianity is unreasonable. You don't have to ask people to close their eyes, cover their ears, and leap into a chasm to become Christians—instead, you ask them to exert the reasonable faith that man is sinful and that Christ died for our sins. Christians ask non-Christians, in effect, to trade in their desperate hope that man is trustworthy for the much more feasible hope that Christ is trustworthy. As C.S. Lewis explains, the non-Christian is "no longer faced with an argument which demands your assent, but with a Person who demands your confidence."[55] And once a person realizes that men tend to betray confidences, it seems eminently reasonable to rely on the only Person worthy of our confidence.

Lewis elsewhere raises another point that bears mentioning. Coming to trust Christ as your Lord and Savior requires just a bit of reasonable faith, but once you've trusted Him you may find that He expects a much bigger faith from you. This new demand for faith still won't ask you to blind yourself—it's never irrational to trust in an all-powerful, perfectly holy God—but it may require you to follow Him in a direction you don't like and for which you can't imagine a purpose. Lewis describes this type of faith this way:

> There are times when we can do all that a
> fellow creature needs if only he will trust us.
> In getting a dog out of a trap, in extracting a
> thorn from a child's finger, in teaching a boy to
> swim or rescuing one who can't, in getting a

frightened beginner over a nasty place on a mountain, the one fatal obstacle may be their distrust. We are asking them to trust us in the teeth of their senses, their imagination, and their intelligence. We ask them to believe that what is painful will relieve their pain and that what looks dangerous is their only safety. . . . Sometimes, because of their unbelief, we can do no mighty works. But if we succeed, we do so because they have maintained their faith in us against apparently contrary evidence. No one blames us for demanding such faith. No one blames them for giving it. No one says afterwards what an unintelligent dog or child or boy that must have been to trust us. If the young mountaineer were a scientist, it would not be held against him, when he came up for a fellowship, that he had once departed from Clifford's rule of evidence by entertaining a belief with strength greater than the evidence logically obliged him to.

Now to accept the Christian propositions is *ipso facto* to believe that we are to God, always, as that dog or child or bather or mountain climber was to us, only very much more so.[56]

We don't always understand the situations in which we find ourselves. At these times, the wisest course of action is not to trust our own instincts, but instead to trust God. When you're really scared, it may seem that this requires a great deal of faith—but it is still much more *reasonable* to trust the Creator of the universe than our own panicked and imperfect emotions. God only asks us to follow Him, which, when you think about it, makes a lot more sense than trusting ourselves.

It is often difficult for Christians to follow, however, when the world keeps telling them to keep their faith to themselves. When most people act as though Christianity is applicable only to "church matters," many Christians find it hard to remember that God expects them to apply their faith to every aspect of reality.

Sayers says that "What we in fact believe is not necessarily the theory we most desire or admire. It is the thing that, consciously or unconsciously, we take for granted and act on."[57] Christians say, of course, that they believe the Bible—but in modern times we too often "take for granted" the worldly belief that our faith only applies in certain areas—that there is a distinction between the sacred and the secular. Too often, Christians assume the worldly attitude modeled by one of Sayers' characters when he says that "Religion's a bit out of my line, except on Sundays."[58]

Christianity can never be "out of our line." Christ warns us that "If anyone would come after me, he must deny himself and take up his cross daily and follow me" (Luke 9:23). Not just on Sundays. Not just in church. Every day and in every way, Christians are commanded to follow Christ.

This means being bold enough to apply our faith in the classroom, in Congress, or in a foxhole. It means being unashamed of our commitment to the Savior Who sacrificed Himself for us. We need to take seriously the warning that Christ sounded shortly after telling His followers to pick up their crosses: "If anyone is ashamed of me and my words, the

Son of Man will be ashamed of him when he comes in his glory and in the glory of the Father and of the holy angels" (Luke 9:26).

The Christian is called to think, and act, in accord with his worldview all the time. We must learn to apply our faith to every arena, not just the so-called "sacred" arenas. Anything less, as Dietrich Bonhoeffer points out, is schizophrenic:

> The division of the total reality into a sacred and a profane sphere, a Christian and a secular sphere, creates the possibility of existence in a single one of these spheres, a spiritual existence which has no part in secular existence, and a secular existence which can claim autonomy for itself and can exercise this right of autonomy in its dealings with the spiritual sphere.[59]

Accepting the false distinction between faith and reason, or the sacred and the secular, leads to one of two extremes: either false monasticism or a Sunday school Christian. That is, either a Christian tries to lock himself away from the world in a hermitage (spending all his time in what he considers a "sacred" arena), or a Christian tries to lock his faith in the church (spending virtually all of his time in what he considers a "secular" arena). Christians are commanded to seek balance between these extremes, being "in the world" but not "of the world" (John 17:15-18).

The way to achieve this is to treat every aspect of reality as "sacred," as something that matters to God. We must recognize, as Bonhoeffer did, that

> There are not two realities, but only one reality,
> and that is the reality of God, which has
> become manifest in Christ in the reality of the
> world. Sharing in Christ we stand at once in
> both the reality of God and the reality of the
> world. . . . There are, therefore, not two
> spheres, but only the one sphere of the realiza-
> tion of Christ, in which the reality of God and
> the reality of the world are united.[60]

And elsewhere he says, "Whoever professes to believe in the reality of Jesus Christ, as the revelation of God, must in the same breath profess his faith in both the reality of God and the reality of the world; for in Christ he finds God and the world reconciled."[61]

Once we understand this truth, we recognize that this is a powerful apologetic for Christianity. "Christian theology," says Lewis, "can fit in science, art, morality, and the sub-Christian religions. . . . I believe in Christianity as I believe that the Sun has risen, not because I see it, but because by it I see everything else."[62] When one begins to understand Christianity as a reasonable faith applicable to all of reality, it becomes much easier to defend your faith when talking with non-Christians.

But don't spend all your time defending your faith. Ask others—gently—to defend their faith, too. Ask them if it's reasonable to believe that man is basically good, and to con-clude that man can save himself. Ask them if the worldview that results from their faith matches reality. The best defense, as every football coach in the world has opined, is a good offense.

This offensive move is not offensive, in the bad sense, because it will help you understand what other people believe, and why they think the way they do. Non-Christians will appreciate your willingness to hear their side of the story and this, in turn, will allow you to implement some good advice from Pascal:

> When we want to correct someone usefully and show him he is wrong, we must see from what point of view he is approaching the matter, for it is usually right from that point of view, and we must admit this, but show him the point of view from which it is wrong. This will please him, because he will see that he was not wrong but merely failed to see every aspect of the question.[63]

In many ways, that's what this book is about. As members of the Hyde crowd, Christians must understand what they believe and then also understand what the rest of the world believes. If we can see from their perspective—the belief that the monster of Frankenstein is real—then we can begin to understand why they believe what they believe in any arena, from astrology to zoology. And once we understand how their faith assumptions color their beliefs, we can help them begin to question those faith assumptions and consider how they might think differently if they believed man was inherently sinful.

The next three chapters will focus specifically on the way the Frankenstein crowd's faith affects their efforts to change themselves and society to work out their salvation. This discussion will carry us from ethics to education to government to psychology, and on the way we'll meet some of the leaders in the war of ideas. The final chapter will consider man without monsters, discussing the role of men and women who have seen their Hyde nailed to the cross.

As we proceed, the differences between Christianity and all other worldviews will continue to crop up like dandelions, revealing incessantly that Christianity is both radically different and true. The bankruptcy of all other worldviews will sprawl before you as it did before Levin, an autobiographical character in Leo Tolstoy's classic *Anna Karenin*:

> For him the problem was this: 'If I do not accept the answers Christianity gives to the questions of my life, what answers do I accept?' And in the whole arsenal of his convictions he failed to find not only any kind of answer but anything resembling an answer. He was in the position of a man seeking food in a toyshop or at a gunsmith's.[64]

If man is capable of saving himself, well and good—let him go about the business of answering life's questions. But if man can't save himself, as the world's whole history seems to attest, let us place our faith in the One who can save us, and follow Him across any and every boundary marked "sacred" or "secular."

BLIND FAITH

"If he exalts himself, I humble him.
If he humbles himself, I exalt him.
And I go on contradicting him
Until he understands
That he is a monster that passes all understanding."
—Blaise Pascal

CHAPTER 3

ON OUR BEST BEHAVIOR

I n addition to flying kites, writing almanacs and lobbying for independence, Benjamin Franklin liked to tinker with morality. His most famous experiment was also his most ambitious: an effort to perfect himself by defining morality and rigorously focusing on his moral improvement every day. "I wished to live," he says, "without committing any fault at any time; I would conquer all that either natural inclination, custom, or company might lead me into."[2]

Franklin decided that attaining perfection required practicing thirteen specific virtues consistently: temperance, silence, order, resolution, frugality, industry, sincerity, justice, moderation, cleanliness, tranquillity, chastity, and humility.

"I judged it would be well," writes Franklin, "not to distract my attention by attempting the whole at once but to fix it on one of them at a time, and when I should be master of that, then to proceed to another, and so on till I should have gone thro' the thirteen."[3] Toward this end, Franklin chose one virtue to master, and began keeping a detailed scorecard to record his successes and failures.

Franklin's allegiance to Frankenstein shines through this experiment. As he admits, he expected himself to know the good and to be capable of doing good: "As I knew, or thought I knew, what was right and wrong, I did not see why I might not *always* do the one and avoid the other."[4]

This assumption follows logically from Franklin's faith in the goodness of man, and so it was reasonable for him, based on his worldview, to hope that his experiment would succeed. Likewise, anyone sharing Franklin's faith in man might expect good results. Certainly no one could ask for a better guinea pig for the experiment: Franklin was an inventor, statesman, and genius. His attention to detail in this area was assiduous, and he persevered in his experiment for many years.

And yet, after all those years, it was the Hyde crowd's faith that was validated. All of Franklin's perseverance and all of his genius couldn't put man back together again. As Franklin admits, he discovered almost immediately that he was in over his head: "I soon found I had undertaken a task of more difficulty than I had imagined. While my attention was taken up and care employed in guarding against one fault, I was often surprized by another. . . . Inclination was sometimes too strong for reason."[5] His hard work did, of course, result in improvement ("I was surprized to find myself so much fuller of faults than I had imagined, but I had the satisfaction of seeing them diminish."[6]), but still left him "far short" of "the perfection I had been so ambitious of obtaining."[7] He confessed a real incapacity for being orderly, and he could not juggle all thirteen virtues at once—he could only be virtuous in certain ways at certain times.

As a man with a high opinion of himself, Franklin didn't take his failure too hard. In fact, he wondered if his failure to achieve moral perfection might, in itself, be a good thing:

> Something that pretended to be reason was
> ever now and then suggesting to me that such
> extreme nicety as I exacted of myself might be

a kind of foppery in morals, which if it were
known would make me ridiculous; that a
perfect character might be attended with the
inconvenience of being envied and hated; and
that a benevolent man would allow a few faults
in himself, to keep his friends in countenance.[8]

Since being too good might cause others to feel badly about
themselves, he reasoned, it might be better to not be so good!

Before we laugh at Franklin's conclusion, however, we should
remember that we, too, hate to be "goody two-shoes," and that all
of us sometimes claim that our own moral flaws make us more
endearing. The reason I mention Franklin's experiment is not to
point out his absurd preference for imperfection over perfection
(this absurdity is common to every man), but rather to consider
what type of ethical system must naturally follow from the
assumption that man is basically good.

The way you act flows naturally from what you believe—
your worldview. As we continue our comparison of the
Christian worldview with all other ideologies, then, we should
take time to compare Christian morality with non-Christian
morality. As we consider these differences, keep a few questions in mind: Whose ethical system conforms better with
reality, and seems more humane? Whose morality is consistent
and profound?

PRIDE AND SELFISHNESS AS VIRTUES

Franklin's experiment is a terrific starting point because, as
a deist, Franklin considers ethics from the same perspective as

all other members of the Frankenstein crowd. He begins where unredeemed man always begins, trying to rescue himself by his own power. Franklin explicitly does what every non-Christian implicitly does: he starts with the assumption that man is basically good, and then seeks to use that goodness to perfect himself, to achieve his own salvation.

A moment's reflection, however, reveals that this mentality is both prideful and selfish. In order to believe that you can perfect yourself, you must have an extraordinarily high opinion of yourself. You must believe that you are capable of avoiding all the temptation and negative environmental influences that cause your brethren to stumble every day. You must believe that you have the ability and the will power to be as pure as a mountain stream, shunning every bad thought, word, and action. *And* you must believe that you have an unerring, built-in sense of what is right and what is wrong. Put simply, you must be pretty special.

This pride must co-exist with a strong tendency toward selfishness. If the knowledge of right and wrong exists within you, then you should turn your eyes inward to avoid being led astray. The man in charge of working out his own salvation must work on *himself* first and last, because he is responsible for whether or not he reaches perfection. Your focus, whether you are on a quiet path or in a burning building, must be on your own intuition and your own redemption.

Now, if man really is basically good, such pride and selfishness are justified. It's not prideful to believe you're pure if you really are pure, and it wouldn't be wrong to keep your eyes focused on yourself if you knew you could always trust yourself to do good. In fact, if the Frankenstein crowd is right about the nature of man, this type of pride and this type of selfishness are actually *virtues*, since man needs to act in this way to redeem himself. Pride and selfishness are only vices if the Hyde crowd is right when they say that man is merely a created being in rebellion against his holy Creator.

Interestingly, Franklin's list of virtues originally numbered only twelve. He did not add the thirteenth virtue, humility, until a Quaker friend suggested that he might need to work on that, too. Although Franklin acceded, he never really succeeded at learning this virtue. He writes, "I cannot boast of much success in acquiring the *reality* of this virtue, but I had a good deal with regard to the *appearance* of it."[9]

We should not be surprised. Someone who believes that he is basically good need not see any problems with being prideful and selfish. These "virtues" follow logically from that faith assumption. Or perhaps it would be more accurate to say that the faith assumption follows logically from man's tendency toward pride and selfishness. The Bible makes it clear that pride and selfishness caused the fall of Adam, and that these vices lie at the very core of every unredeemed man. Really, we find ourselves facing a "chicken or egg" dilemma when we discuss which came first, unredeemed man's belief that he is basically good, or his tendency toward pride and selfishness. It was Adam's pride and selfishness that caused him to believe that he could be like God, and it was his belief that he could be like God that caused him to curse all his descendants with inherent pride and selfishness.

Pride and selfishness are so entangled with the belief that man is basically good that they are effectively inseparable and often indistinguishable. Dorothy Sayers equates pride and selfishness with faith in man when she says that pride

113

is the sin of trying to be as God. It is the sin that proclaims that man can produce out of his own wits, and his own impulses, and his own imagination the standards by which he lives: that man is fitted to be his own judge. . . . The name under which pride walks the world at this moment is the perfectibility of man, or the doctrine of progress; and its specialty is the making of blueprints for utopia and establishing the kingdom of man on earth.[10]

Satan sold pride and selfishness as virtues in the Garden of Eden, and man has been corrupted by them, and blind to this corruption, ever since.

Still, you may find it hard to believe that anyone would describe pride or selfishness as a virtue. Everybody you know says, "Don't be selfish," and talks as though they appreciate humility. This is generally true—many non-Christians would never use the words *pride* or *selfishness* in a positive light. Instead, these non-Christians use less emotionally-charged words like *self-esteem, self-actualization, respect*, and *personal worth*. They don't tell others to be selfish; instead, they urge them to feel good about themselves. Their words are different, but their meaning is the same. As William Kilpatrick reminds us, "Most of us know . . . that 'feeling good about myself' is sometimes a handy excuse for doing self-centered or even selfish things."[11] If you believe that man is basically good, then you must view pride and selfishness as ethical imperatives (whether you use those specific terms or not).

I'm going to set aside the whole sticky self-esteem discussion until the following chapter, where we delve deeper into psychology. For now, we'll concentrate on the two possible ethical systems man can adopt, and in order to keep things clear we will hear only from members of the Frankenstein crowd who specifically encourage people to be prideful and selfish (you'll be surprised how many there are). To further simplify, we will treat the terms *pride* and *selfishness* as interchangeable—since they are really two sides of the same coin. To be prideful is to think highly of self, and to be selfish is to believe that you're important enough to merit close attention. It doesn't matter whether we label Adam's original sin as an act of pride or an act of selfishness, because it was actually both. Likewise, whenever we find members of the Frankenstein crowd championing pride as a virtue, you can be certain that they encourage selfishness as well, or vice versa. From this point forward, then, when I refer to the virtue of selfishness, I mean the virtues of both pride and selfishness.

THE ETHICS OF FRANKENSTEIN

The first of the two possible ethical systems that man can adopt is the Frankenstein system. *Every human being* starts with this system, because every human starts as a member of the Frankenstein crowd, seeking to work out his or her own salvation. Different non-Christian worldviews may seem to prescribe radically different ethics, but a closer examination reveals that all non-Christians—from atheists to Hindus to Muslims—ultimately share the same ethical conclusions and attitudes. The first and best example of this is the unreserved adoption, by every non-Christian worldview, of the virtue of selfishness. Man must rely on himself to know, and to do, the good.

It's fairly easy to see why atheistic worldviews call for men to practice this virtue. Once a person has accepted the idea that man is only a highly evolved animal with no transcendent purpose, it seems pretty logical for that person to believe that the best thing they can do is look out for themselves. The extreme example of the atheists' adoption of a selfish ethic is provided by those men and women who applied Charles Darwin's ideas about survival of the fittest to mankind (especially Adolf Hitler, Edmund Spencer and Margaret Sanger). According to this view, the wisest thing any person can do is take care of themselves so that they can live through the struggle for existence. The ruthlessness of this creed (and its tendency to incorporate racism) is best expressed in a prediction made by Darwin himself: "Looking to the world at no very distant date, what an endless number of the lower races will have been eliminated by the higher civilized races throughout the world."[12] Assuming this prediction is accurate, it would make a lot of sense to practice the virtue of selfishness, taking care not to be eliminated.

It's also fairly easy to see why New Age proponents encourage men to be selfish. If man is really god, then the wisest thing man can do is get in touch with his godhood by focusing on himself (whether through meditation, hypnosis, firewalking, or other occultic practices). Thus, we should not be too surprised to hear Shirley MacLaine say, "I was beginning to see that we each did whatever we did purely for self, and that was as it should be."[13] According to Kilpatrick, the selfishness of the New Age proponent is "quite logical" for another reason as well, because "if one's self is coextensive with the universe then the problem of loving others is solved by loving one's self. Why bother with the others if you're a universe unto yourself?"[14]

According to the New Age worldview, the worst thing that can happen to a person is for that person to give up their own authority and allow some other authority (like the state, church, or family) to set limits on their lives. According to this view, the self should be the only authority because every self is god, and we only lose touch with our godhood when we let ourselves be limited. For example, New Age author Shakti Gawain warns that "If you're setting limits on your sexual energy, it becomes distorted."[15] The way to behave properly is to focus on yourself and make sure that you get your way all the time.

Logically, then, selfishness becomes a virtue for the New Age and atheistic worldviews. And perhaps Franklin's experiment makes it credible that deism also encourages this focus on self. But what about Judaism, Mormonism or Islam? What about worldviews with sacred scriptures and purported revelations from God? These religions often prescribe specific moral codes that require a great deal of effort, and they often require adherents to do good for others and for their community. Certainly one cannot say that a Mormon praying for his kindred dead is practicing the virtue of selfishness?

This is precisely what I'm saying. The Mormon, the Jew, the Buddhist, and every other believer in Frankenstein must find the ability to rescue themselves within them-selves. This means, practically, that every good deed they perform helps them save their own skin. The Mormon may claim that he is praying for his kindred dead based on purely selfless motives, but the fact remains that he cannot be exalted without offering up these prayers. Likewise, the Jehovah's Witness seems to be doing an unselfish thing by sharing his faith with others, but unless he does so he can never be saved. The underlying motive for every "ought" in every non-Christian religion is selfishness, because you can't risk your own salvation by spending too much time thinking about other people—you've got to concentrate on rescuing yourself.

Siddhartha Gautama, the man known as Buddha, provides perhaps the best example. Before he became enlightened, he experimented with different lifestyles in an effort to find the way to save himself. He eventually chose to leave his wife so that he could seek the path to redemption more zealously. This selfish desertion was completely consistent with his belief that he had to rescue himself, because he couldn't allow even his wife's needs to thwart his own efforts to get enlightened.

Does your wife get in the way of your quest for salvation? If it's true that you can save yourself, you'd better ditch her and focus on living the proper life. Is your job in the way, or your dog, or your best friend? Get rid of them! If your salvation depends on your own goodness, you'd better focus on yourself and cast all loyalty aside. Loyalty is a nice sentiment, but it certainly can't take precedence over achieving salvation.

None of this means, of course, that every non-Christian acts selfishly all the time. Most non-Christians occasionally sacrifice their own interests in fits of compassion, and many will occasionally choose loyalty over achieving salvation (even though such a choice is irrational). Selfishness is not the only motive for the non-Christian, and Christians are not immune from selfish motivations. The difference between non-Christians and Christians is *not* that one acts selfishly all the time and one does not, but rather that one will often treat selfishness as a virtue while the other views selfishness only as a vice.

MODERN EXAMPLES

One of the best indications that members of the Frankenstein crowd are willing to treat selfishness as a virtue is the fact that two such people actually collaborated on a book entitled *The Virtue of Selfishness.* Ayn Rand and her disciple, Nathaniel Branden, contend in this book that faith in man requires men to trust themselves and act with their own interests in mind. These authors not only promote selfishness; they also go out of their way to attack acts of self-sacrifice. Rand says it is "indecent" that "A young man who gives up his career in order to support his parents and never rises beyond the rank of grocery clerk is regarded as morally superior to the young man who endures an excruciating struggle and achieves his personal ambition."[16]

Branden tries desperately to dismiss self-sacrificial acts as nothing more than covert selfishness:

> [L]et us consider an extreme example of an action which, in fact, is selfish, but which conventionally might be called self-sacrificial: a man's willingness to die to save the life of the woman he loves. In what way would such a man be the beneficiary of his action? . . . If a man loves a woman so much that he does not wish to survive her death, if life can have nothing more to offer him at that price, then his dying to save her is not a sacrifice.[17]

He goes on to say that "The same principle applies to a man, caught in a dictatorship, who willingly risks death to achieve freedom. To call his act a 'self-sacrifice,' one would have to assume that he *preferred* to live as a slave."[18] This assumption is unmerited, according to Branden, and so the man's sacrifice is really selfish.

According to Branden's logic, then, it would seem that everyone acts primarily due to selfish motives. Not so, he says. He acknowledges that all men have a superficial selfishness, but he laments that many do not possess "genuine selfishness," which he describes as "a genuine concern with discovering what is to one's self-interest, an acceptance of the responsibility of achieving it, a refusal ever to betray it by acting on the blind whim, mood, impulse or feeling of the moment, an uncompromising loyalty to one's judgment, convictions and values." This true selfishness, according to Branden, is "a profound moral achievement."[19]

Countless other non-Christians are willing to describe selfishness as a moral achievement. Ramana Maharshi, a Hindu known as "the greatest holy man of modern India," tells his disciples that holy men need not reach out to others because "The Self is the only Reality." Maharshi says that helping others is God's job: "If God has created the world, it is His business to look after it, not yours."[20] Abraham Maslow recommends selfishness when he says, "Since [man's] inner nature is good or neutral rather than bad, it is best to bring it out and to encourage it rather than to suppress it. If it is permitted to guide our life, we grow healthy, fruitful, and happy."[21] Erich Fromm attacks self-sacrifice:

> 'Don't be selfish' is a sentence which has been
> impressed upon millions of children, genera-

tion after generation. . . . Aside from its obvious implication, it means, 'don't love yourself,' 'don't be yourself,' but submit yourself to something more important than yourself, to an outside power or its internalization, 'duty.' 'Don't be selfish' becomes one of the most powerful ideological tools in suppressing spontaneity and the free development of personality. Under the pressure of this slogan one is asked for every sacrifice and for complete submission: only those acts are 'unselfish' which do not serve the individual but somebody or something outside himself.[22]

This attitude of some of the most popular psychologists in recent history led to the '60s self-help movement and the "I'm okay, you're okay" generation. The mantra of this generation was Fritz Perls' "Gestalt Prayer," perhaps the ultimate selfishness credo:

I do my thing
And you do your thing.
I am not in the world to live up to your expectations,
And you are not in the world to live up to mine.
You are you and I am I,
And if by chance we find each other, it's beautiful.
If not, it can't be helped.

Though this mentality may have reached its peak in the
'60s, it is still alive and well today—and not just for psychologists in ivory towers. The fact that the virtue of selfishness is
assumed by everyday men and women is amply demonstrated
by a recent letter to the editor in my local newspaper:

> Why is it that on every Mother's Day, mothers
> are forced by their children and husbands to go
> places they don't want to go, eat food they
> hate, see movies or shows that the children or
> Dad choose (Mom might want to see a ro-
> mance or a musical) and smile sweetly and
> express intense gratitude while they are being
> abused mentally and emotionally in the name
> of Mother's Day? Why can't mothers demand
> exactly what the family will do for them on
> Mother's Day? After all, every day is Kid's Day
> and Father's Day. Mother's Day is just another
> way of torturing women while pretending to
> love them (so what else is new).[23]

Translation: Mothers can only be fulfilled when their needs are
met, not when they are meeting others' needs. Mothers should
be selfish, too.

THE ETHICS OF HYDE

The Hyde crowd says exactly the opposite. While Christians admit that preoccupation with self is common to every
man, the elevation of selfishness to a virtue is a specifically
non-Christian phenomenon. You ought to look out for

number one? Not according to Christ. "For whoever wants to save his life will lose it, but whoever loses his life for me will find it" (Matthew 16:25). As Dietrich Bonhoeffer says, "When Christ calls a man, he bids him come and die."[24]

When Karl Marx was an old man, one of his daughters persuaded him to fill out a questionnaire that included the question, "Which vice do you detest most?" Marx wrote down the word *servility*.[25] Not surprisingly, the Christian ethical system begins right at the place Marx and the rest of the Frankenstein crowd say we should avoid: self-sacrifice. While the world says it is good to focus on ourselves, Christ says that the two greatest goods involve focusing on God and on other people (Matthew 22:34-40). Non-Christians build their ethical systems on the underlying imperative to be selfish; Christ builds His ethical system on the underlying imperative to be *selfless*.

The Frankenstein crowd predicts that we must love ourselves before we can love God or our neighbors, but the Hyde crowd warns frankly that "you can't get there from here." Christians recognize that those who start with loving themselves can never tear their eyes away from the mirror, as Pascal explains: "The nature of self-love and of this human self is to love only self and consider only self."[26]

As you might expect, B.F. Skinner understands the enormous "perspective gap" between the ethics of Hyde and that of Frankenstein. In *Walden Two*, Skinner makes his autobiographical character, Frazier, ask, "What is love, except another name for the use of positive reinforcement?"[27] For Skinner, love is only a method we use to cause others to behave in a way that pleases us. Love is selfish. For the Christian, as Ravi Zacharias says, "[T]he opposite of love is selfishness."[28] The Christian concept of love is as different from the world's as giving is from taking:

> Love is patient, love is kind. It does not envy, it does not boast, it is not proud. It is not rude, it is not self-seeking, it is not easily angered, it keeps no record of wrongs. Love does not delight in evil but rejoices with the truth. It always protects, always trusts, always hopes, always perseveres. Love never fails. (1 Corinthians 13:4-8)

Love, for the Christian, is synonymous with selflessness. When Christ says, "Greater love has no one than this, that he lay down his life for his friends" (John 15:13), Christians assume that Christ is talking about his sacrificial death on the cross—as He certainly is. But He is also talking about what He expects from His friends. Yes, Christ sacrificed His life for us—and now He expects us to do the same for Him! Friendship really is a two-way street. Christ makes this clear when he follows this statement with a reminder (in verse 17) that we are commanded to "Love each other." Anyone doubtful about what love means can refer back to His definition: laying down your life.

This holds true whether we consider Christ's own life or the lives of Stephen, Paul, Peter, or modern martyrs. The world will know we are Christians by our love—not our love for self, but our love for God and for our neighbor. "Genuine love," says Bonhoeffer, "is always self-forgetful."[29]

This morality goes against everything dear to natural man. As sinners, we want to be in charge, to be "free" to rebel against God whenever we like. "The natural life in each of us," according to C.S. Lewis,

> is something self-centered, something that wants to be petted and admired, to take advantage of other lives, to exploit the whole universe. And specially it wants to be left to itself: to keep well away from anything better or stronger or higher than it, anything that might make it feel small. It's afraid of the light and air of the spiritual world, just as people who've been brought up to be dirty are afraid of a bath. And in a sense it's quite right. It knows that if the spiritual life gets hold of it, all its self-centeredness and self-will are going to be killed and it's ready to fight tooth and nail to avoid *that*.[30]

Unredeemed man would much rather believe in the virtue of selfishness than risk dying to his own desires and following Christ. But the death of our sinful selves is exactly what God requires; as Lewis says, you must "Die before you die. There is no chance after."[31]

DYING DAILY

At this point, it is imperative that we be clear: for the Christian, death happens once, twice, and daily. In the physical realm, we die once, and after that face the judgment (Hebrews 9:27). Overall, Christians die twice—once physically, and once before that when our sinful selves face a spiritual death as we are "crucified with Christ" (Galatians 2:20) and born again. This spiritual re-birth, when a man passes from death to life not by his own power but because of Christ's work on the cross, is a one-time event. We don't need to be saved every day, and we don't need to work hard to ensure our salvation, because Christ's work on the cross is sufficient. If man can't save himself, then neither can he re-save himself. Our salvation is not secured by our right living (thank God), but by the right living of the only perfect sacrifice, Jesus Christ. None of our puny failings are big enough to render such a sacrifice null or void. What's more, since the Christian does not save himself, he can take no pride in the fact that he was saved. People don't go to heaven because they were smart enough to see that they were sinful or because they were brave enough to trust Christ. They go to heaven because God, in His grace, allowed them to go to heaven. The work of salvation is God's work alone, as Paul explains in Colossians 2:13: "When you were dead in your sins and in the uncircumcision of your sinful nature, God made you alive with Christ."

The third kind of death—daily death—is what Christ expects of us now. This is the ethic of selflessness, an ethic that requires renewed commitment every day. Our proper response to our Creator and Redeemer is to lay down our lives, pick up our crosses, and follow Him. We must relinquish all control and trust Him as our Guide. This means, as Charles Colson says, that we must cease to measure success in the worldly way—fame, money, power, happiness, playing second base for the Cleveland Indians—and instead define success as *obedience*. "It is not what we do that matters, *but what a sovereign God chooses to do through us.* God doesn't want our success; He wants us. He doesn't demand our achievements; He demands our obedience."[32] Living selflessly is wise, because it entrusts the Perfect One rather than imperfect man with the direction for our lives, but it is also proper, because all good things come from God. To expect to find goodness within ourselves is hopeless—if we are to glorify God, we must do so by His own power.

Once a man becomes a Christian, he must get on with the everyday business of following Christ—a business that will be marked by failures. Just because the Hyde crowd recognizes their sinful tendencies and understands the need to act selflessly doesn't mean that we will act selflessly all the time. People who trust Christ aren't perfect—just *free*. We may use our freedom from sin to follow Christ, but we may also choose to quench the Holy Spirit and act sinfully. The choice is ours, every day—and what is required from us is total surrender of our wills to God. The only way to lead a completely righteous life is to make your self-sacrifice complete, each day. Lewis explains,

> Christ says, 'Give me *all*. I don't want so much
> of your time and so much of your money and
> so much of your work: I want *you*. I have not
> come to torment your natural self, but to kill
> it. No half-measures are any good. I don't
> want to cut off a branch here and a branch
> there, I want to have the whole tree down'.[33]

The felling of the tree, so to speak, is the point of the Christian life on earth. Christians still like to feel like they are in control of parts of their lives—but we must get to the point where

Christ is in control of everything. In heaven, we will have surrendered completely—and we should be preparing for that total surrender right now:

> The terrible thing, the almost impossible thing, is to hand over your whole self—all your wishes and precautions—to Christ. But it's far easier than what we're all trying to do instead. For what we're trying to do is to remain what we call 'ourselves,' to keep personal happiness as our great aim in life, and yet at the same time be 'good.' We're all trying to let our mind and heart go their own way—centered on money or pleasure or ambition—and hoping, in spite of this, to behave honestly and chastely and humbly. And that is exactly what Christ warned us you couldn't do. As He said, a thistle can't produce figs.[34]

> It's been said, and wisely so, that the problem with a living sacrifice is that it keeps crawling off the altar. You might, on your best day, almost completely forget about your own desires and make sacrifices for God and your neighbor. But just because you're successful that day doesn't mean you'll be successful every day. Each morning we must consciously pick up our self and put it back on the altar. Like lighthouse keepers, the toughest part of our work is the vigilance—doing our duty every day and night, even when we don't feel like it, for years and years. "There is nowhere this side of heaven," says Lewis, "where one can safely lay the reins on the horse's neck."[35] Christians must work hard today

and then, whether we ride or are thrown, dust ourselves off and work hard again tomorrow.

The metaphors of the altar, the lighthouse, and horseback riding are all imperfect, of course, because they make it sound like redeemed man can be good based on his own hard work. As Dr. Jekyll demonstrates, man cannot be good on his own. Whenever you behave selflessly, the real work is done by the Holy Spirit—you have only stepped out of the way. Redeemed man does the work of dodging aside, so that the good can be done by the One Who is good.

For the Christian, the news just keeps getting better and better. We begin with the bad news that we're like Hyde, but that leads us to the tremendous news that a perfect sacrifice has been provided for us because God loves us so very much. Our Savior then bids us to follow Him, which seems like a hard thing—until we recognize that He will supply all the strength and all the courage required of us. Life in this world may be hard for the Christian, but if we will humble ourselves and cling to Christ, we will find ourselves safe in the arms of the One who has "overcome the world" (John 16:33). The only thing required of us is to let Him be in control.

As Christians practice getting out of the way—allowing ourselves to be led by the Spirit—we will find that the hard work of following Christ grows a little easier. Self-sacrifice may never seem like a "natural" thing until we get to heaven, but sacrifices can flow a little easier as we stop trying to cap the Spirit and instead let His work gush out of us (John 7:38-39). As Sayers explains, Christians usually start making sacrifices out of duty and eventually learn to make sacrifices out of love:

When one really cares, the self is forgotten, and
the sacrifice becomes only a part of the activity.
Ask yourself: if there is something you supremely want to do, do you count as
self-sacrifice the difficulties encountered or the
other possible activities cast aside? You do not.
The time when you deliberately say, 'I must
sacrifice this, that, or the other' is when you do
not supremely desire the end in view. At such
times you are doing your duty, and that is
admirable, but it is not love. But as soon as
your duty becomes your love the self-sacrifice is
taken for granted, and, whatever the world
calls it, you call it so no longer.[36]

When Christians grow in Christ and learn to sacrifice not
only out of duty but also out of love, their lives may demonstrate the radical difference between the Christian ethical
system and the ethics that result from the Frankenstein view.[37]
As we grant more and more control to God, we can live in
such a way that our lives become an apologetic for the truth of
Christianity.

Most of us have heard non-Christians argue that Christianity can't be true because Christians are just as bad as everyone
else. If Christians have been "born again," the world argues,
why do they look and act like everyone else?

This is a fair question, and it deserves a fair answer—but
this book can't provide it. Neither can any other book, nor any
other argument. The only sufficient response can't be jotted
down or memorized; it has to be *lived*. This is the sense in
which our lives are an apologetic for our faith. People under-

stand that our actions are determined by our faith, so if they find that our actions are honorable and in step with reality, then our foundation for our actions—our worldview—becomes much more credible. The non-Christian charge that Christians should behave differently is completely justified—we should! And the only way to refute their conclusion that trusting Christ doesn't change lives is to show them that it does.

WALKING THE TALK

Unfortunately, it's a lot easier to talk like a Christian than it is to live like a Christian—as G.K. Chesterton says, "The Christian ideal has not been tried and found wanting. It has been found difficult; and left untried."[38] Our job, as followers of Christ, is to try—to surrender our lives to God so that His power will be manifest through us. Though this is difficult, there is some consolation: we don't have to rely solely on our own actions to demonstrate this. The lives of godly men and women throughout history amply demonstrate the fact that following Christ leads to radically different choices and actions. This holds true for famous Christians like Jonathan Edwards and Elisabeth Eliot, but it also holds true for many unknown individuals. Consider two stories:

When the Los Angeles riots erupted after the Rodney King fiasco, the world was horrified to see innocent men and women beaten and abused simply because they were in the wrong place at the wrong time. Perhaps the most terrifying scene was enacted when a trucker was pulled from the cab of his truck and beaten severely. A television camera captured the scene, so that most Americans saw the grisly drama played out on the evening news. In Los Angeles, however, local television stations provided 24-hour coverage of the riots, so that viewers saw the beating *live*, as it happened.

I don't know how you would have reacted if you found yourself in Los Angeles watching that attack on the trucker, but I know what I would have done: while feeling very sorry for the victim, I would have thanked my lucky stars that I was safe at home and not on the streets where such danger loomed. I suspect that most people would respond the same way. But two people who really were in Los Angeles at that time reacted very differently. Lei Yuille describes what happened when she and her brother witnessed the beating: "My brother was in the room. He looked at me and said, 'We are Christians. We've got to go help him out,' and I said, 'Right.' Then he went and got his keys."[39] Instead of recognizing the danger in the streets and staying cozy and warm on the couch, Lei and her brother risked everything to help a man they didn't know!

Big deal? I'd say so. This one action, performed in the heat of the moment, revealed more about Christian ethics than an encyclopedia ever could. The rest of the world, no matter their worldview, would explain patiently to Lei and her brother that their first responsibility was to themselves; only Christ could expect their reckless willingness to count themselves as nothing. No other worldview would dare require such behavior; only Christ says, "Give me all."

Significantly, even non-Christians recognize that this type of behavior is radically different and worthy of notice. I didn't find out about Lei at church or in a Bible study—I read her quote in an issue of *Newsweek*. Even publications normally hostile toward Christianity cannot ignore cities shining on a hill.

The other story may be less dramatic, but it is no less radical. In 1967, Doug Nichols decided to travel to India as a missionary—an odd choice, considering that he did not speak the language. He expected to overcome this hurdle with the written word, using good translations of Christian tracts and the gospel of John. Unfortunately, things went downhill for Doug, and he soon found himself in a sanitarium with tuberculosis. What could be more discouraging? He had come to minister to the people of India, and instead found himself unwell in an unsanitary place, unable to talk to the doctors, nurses and patients around him. Still worse—because he could not communicate with these people, he could not impress upon them their need for a tract or the gospel of John. No one was willing to read his only means of sharing the gospel with them.

Doug describes what happened next:

> The first few nights, I would wake around 2:00 a.m. coughing. One morning as I was going through my coughing spell, I noticed one of the older (and certainly sicker) patients across the aisle trying to get out of bed. He would sit up on the edge of the bed and try to stand, but because of weakness would fall back into bed. I really didn't understand what was happening or what he was trying to do. He finally fell back into bed exhausted. I then heard him begin to cry softly.
>
> The next morning I realized what the man was trying to do. He was simply trying to get up and walk to the bathroom! Because of his

sickness and extreme weakness he was not able to do this, and being so ill he simply went to the toilet in the bed.

The next morning the stench in our ward was awful. Most of the other patients yelled insults at the man because of the smell. The nurses were extremely agitated and angry because they had to clean up the mess, and moved him roughly from side to side to take care of the problem. One of the nurses in her anger even slapped him. The man, terribly embarrassed, just curled up into a ball and wept.[40]

The same scenario was replayed the next night: Doug was awakened by a coughing spell around two in the morning, and he noticed the same man trying weakly to stand. Without stopping to think about what he was doing, Doug got up, picked up the smaller man, and carried him to the bathroom. After the man finished, Doug returned him to his bed, went back to his own bed, and went to sleep. But he did not sleep long.

At four in the morning, another patient woke Doug and used hand motions to indicate that he wanted one of Doug's tracts. As the morning wore on, more patients, nurses, and doctors indicated that they, too, would like one of Doug's tracts or gospel books—until every person in the hospital had one. Within a few days, several of these same people trusted Christ as their Savior!

Obviously, it wasn't true to say that Doug had no way of communicating with these people. He could use the very best means of communication: his actions. Though Doug couldn't *tell* the people in India that Christ had made a difference in his life, he could *show* them—by humbling himself to the point where he was willing to serve strangers, even in distasteful ways. He showed himself willing to live by the principle in Philippians 2:3, a principle so radical that the rest of the world calls for us to do just the opposite: "Do nothing out of selfish ambition or vain conceit, but in humility consider others better than yourself." Non-Christians always recognize this radical selflessness when they see it, because they spend so much time warning against acting this way (they call it "letting someone take advantage of you").

Christians must understand their worldview, and they must be prepared to defend their faith—but such knowledge means nothing until it is put into practice. To paraphrase Paul, if you can demonstrate that your faith is reasonable and can articulate the differences between your faith and all other faiths, but have not love, you might as well never open your mouth. Let me be plain: if we think and talk like a Christian, but don't care to live like a Christian, we are worse than hypocrites—we are actually stumbling blocks that make it more difficult for others to know Christ. Our words not only become meaningless, but they actually cause others to doubt the veracity of our faith.

The way we live is not just one possible apologetic for Christianity; it is the only indispensable apologetic. Without love, nothing we say or write will influence others to suspect that Christianity might be true; with love, we also have the chance to think and speak in a way that the Holy Spirit can use to lead non-Christians to Him.

J.F. BALDWIN

The rotten core of the ethics of Frankenstein is best exposed not by fine-sounding arguments, but by people like Lei and her brother and Doug. As the world works hard to practice the virtue of selfishness, men will be astounded to find grains of salt in the otherwise flavorless blend of me, me, me, I, I, I. When Christians actually consider others better than themselves, *Newsweek* takes notice and the call to selfishness seems tawdry and cold.

The fundamental impotence of selfishness when contrasted with the dynamism of selflessness, however, is only one problem among many for the ethics of Frankenstein. Not only does the virtue of selfishness tend to discourage noble actions, but it also encourages other moral decisions that create problems of their own.

MORAL RELATIVISM

One such problem is the Frankenstein crowd's tendency toward moral relativism. If you begin with faith in man and then conclude that man should look for the good within himself, conflicts over the definition of *good* arise immediately. If selfishness is a virtue, then we must rely on ourselves to discover what is right, even when our idea of morality differs from another man's. Thus, one man's *good* might be another man's *bad*—and both men, since they are basically good, must be right.

Try thinking like a person who believes in the virtue of selfishness, and consider a basic dilemma: it's your first day on a new job, and you're late for work. As you search desperately for a parking space, you notice an older woman cautiously backing up toward an empty space. Without hesitation, you

136

swerve in front of her and glide quickly into the space she wanted. You hop from your car and dash to your office before she can hit you with her purse.

According to many non-Christians, your action was both right and wrong, depending on perspective. By snatching that parking space, you achieved what you considered to be the good: making the right impression on your new boss. But the older woman felt that she deserved the parking spot, and so she must view your action as bad. Morality becomes *relative* to each individual's interpretation.

Atheists have no qualms about embracing relativism, because they believe that man is the highest being and therefore must be the source for all morality. Max Hocutt, an atheist, explains, "If there is no earthly morality laid up in heaven, by what yardstick will we measure earthly moralities? The answer, of course, is that we should use the same yardstick we use to evaluate any other human artifact: satisfaction of our needs."[41] The signatories of the *Humanist Manifesto II* agree: "Ethics stems from human need and interest."[42] Since human needs differ, people's moral judgments will differ as well. Adherents to the New Age worldview tend to conclude the same thing, since they believe that everyone is god and therefore ethical wisdom resides in every individual.

Other non-Christians would disagree, arguing that morality is not determined by men but by sacred scriptures like the Koran or the Book of Mormon. These men and women, mostly theists or polytheists, contend that they avoid the relativism of the atheist and the New Age proponent because they have an absolute standard for morality. Such a conclusion may seem reasonable, but it ignores one basic fact: every non-Christian worldview except Judaism bids men to follow other men, not God—and men are changeable. If we rely on the moral leadership of mere men, we will find ourselves being at least occasionally inconsistent, as they are inconsistent.

Look at it this way. The orthodox Muslim would claim that Mohammed, as a sinless Prophet and conduit for the Koran, is certainly worthy of emulation. But does this mean that the good Muslim should break treaties, as Mohammed occasionally did? To the extent that someone stakes his morality on the character of Mohammed, that person makes his morality as inconsistent as the actions of a mere man. And inconsistency guarantees moral relativism.

A still better example is provided by the Mormon worldview. While the Mormon would claim that morality is based on God's unchanging nature and is revealed to man through the Bible and the Book of Mormon, a closer examination reveals that Mormon morality is also relative. In the first place, Mormons view the Bible as a corrupted document and therefore not entirely trustworthy[43] (thus, one cannot be sure which morality prescribed by the Bible is correct and which is incorrect). They rely instead on the Book of Mormon (a book based on the authority of a man, Joseph Smith, instead of Jesus Christ) as their best codification of moral absolutes. But even this book, it seems, is subject to interpretation. The leadership of the Mormon church is composed of a Council of Twelve Apostles led by a Prophet, and this Prophet can reveal new "truth" to his church at any time. Moral truth, for the Mormon, changes. The Mormon attitude toward polygamy reflects this relativism: in the 19th century, polygamy was considered a righteous practice by Mormons, but its unpopularity with the United States government encouraged them to change their position. Today, polygamy is generally censured by the Mormon church.

The bottom line? If Christianity is true, only the Christian and the traditional Jew can avoid relativism, because only Christianity and Judaism rely on the revealed Word of the *only* unchanging Being. Christian and Jewish morality can be based upon a reliable foundation, but every other worldview's morality has as its foundation the ideas of a changing being— whether Joseph Smith or Charles Taze Russell or Mary Baker Eddy or, more foundationally, the father of lies. The only members of the Frankenstein crowd who are absolutists in the true sense of the word are the Jewish men and women who believe that the Old Testament is the Word of God.

Clearly, the pitfall of relativism gapes wider than many non-Christians would care to admit—swallowing even Mormons, Muslims, and Jehovah's Witnesses. While many people claim to rely on moral absolutes, very few actually do. The vast majority, whether they like it or not, are stuck with relativism.

Ethical relativism is, by its very nature, as shaky as a coffee addict in the morning. If there is no absolute standard for truth, then no man can ever say for certain whether or not an action or an attitude was the *right* action or attitude. Things may *seem* right, or meet your needs in a certain situation, but nothing can actually *be* the right thing to do. Although the Christian would claim that you never should steal another person's parking place, relativists must invent situations and false dilemmas that imply that it is sometimes right for you to do so (otherwise, an edict against stealing parking places would qualify as a moral absolute). Although it seems intuitively obvious that there are some things that are always the right thing to do (being brave instead of running away, for example), relativists must say only that bravery *seems* to be preferable to cowardice.

Once you accept relativism, you can no longer be outraged by people contradicting what you consider to be moral. Instead, you must be prepared to see morality change, or—as many Darwinists like to say—evolve. This evolution generally takes the form of the powerful people imposing their version of morality on the less powerful, as Kilpatrick notes: "If social and moral judgments are nothing but preferences, the preferences of those with the loudest voices and the most push will come to prevail."[44] If man doesn't have an absolute standard to which he may refer, then he can expect to find himself locked in an ethical "survival of the fittest," where the ethical opinions with the most support kill off all other opinions.[45]

The first people to lose in this struggle to define morality are the helpless, as has been amply demonstrated by *Roe v. Wade*. In America prior to 1973, abortion was illegal—explicitly singled out by the government as wrong. Then suddenly the Supreme Court decided that abortion should be legal, and now many people in our society view abortion as morally acceptable, or even laudable. In a relativistic society, such a flip-flop makes sense. Since truth changes, we can expect things that were once censured to be embraced, and vice versa. But if truth changes, it opens up the whole slippery slope: How do we know that it's okay to kill babies in the womb but it's wrong to kill babies outside of the womb? Maybe it's okay to dispose of *all* unfit humans, including the elderly and the mentally ill. And how do we know that murder itself is ever wrong, regardless of the age, health, or social value of the victim? If moral truth changes, perhaps the day will come when the Supreme Court will legalize all murder. Will such a verdict make murder moral?

Relativism leads to confusion because it offers no unchanging standard to sort out conflicts. The hauntingly Orwellian contradiction in the bumper sticker "Pro-child, Pro-family, Pro-choice" provides a good example of the way relativism can muddle a mind. New Age proponent Marianne Williamson describes this confusion in great detail when she considers whether or not abortion is moral:

> Abortion is a tragedy. That doesn't mean it shouldn't be legal—I think it should—but that still doesn't mean it's not a tragedy. We have never come to terms with the fact that for the first time in our social history millions of women turned away their children. And we did do that, girls. There is no pretending that we didn't. There are certain times when we think maybe we shouldn't have, times when we wish with anguish that we hadn't, and times when we have seen, and still see, no other way of proceeding. However we see it, guilt is not helpful. It is not a part of God's vision. No one is guilty, but lots of us are sad.
>
> Don't get waylaid by politics or swayed by false religion. Stay close to your heart, where your feelings are honest and authentic and raw. Abortion is a bitch. Scream and yell at all you have lost, cry and mourn over what you are doing, but never pretend it's a casual thing. It is not. It is a mother saying goodbye to her child and a woman declining a miracle. Talk to God. Talk only to God. Mourn your lost children. Pray for an easier world.[46]

Does Williamson think abortion is morally acceptable? I have no idea. We are confused about her ethics because she is confused about her ethics, because they have no unchanging basis. Relativism poisons any serious discussion of ethics because it deals only in opinions.

INTOLERANT TOLERANCE

Besides relativism, and besides the impotence of selfishness, still another problem haunts the Frankenstein crowd. Embracing the virtue of selfishness almost always leads to ethical relativism, which in turn often leads to intolerant tolerance.

Naturally, those in the Frankenstein crowd do not refer to their tolerance as *intolerant*—they are much more prone to slap that label on Christians. Most non-Christians loudly proclaim their own tolerance because they think that tolerance can solve much of the confusion created by their relativism. Unfortunately, it really only makes things more confusing.

As soon as a relativist begins to recognize that relativism creates conflicts that it cannot resolve, he begins to cast about for another way to resolve them. Often, this search leads the non-Christian to elevate one of his moral preferences to the status of an absolute (even though he has no unchanging basis for this absolute). The moral preference most often elevated to absolute status today is *tolerance*.

Think back again to our dilemma in the parking lot. Who was right and who was wrong? The relativist simply doesn't know—unless he applies his new-found absolute standard of tolerance to the dilemma. Once he does so, it seems clear that the person running late was wrong to take the parking space, because *he has imposed his moral judgment on another person,* namely the older woman. By forcing his morality (namely, his belief that it's morally acceptable to take another person's parking place) on another person, the parking lot thief has *failed to tolerate* the moral beliefs of the older woman, and therefore behaved badly.

According to this view, intolerance is the chief sin. You may do whatever you like, whenever you like, as long as your actions don't impose your morality on another person. As soon as you overstep this absolute boundary, however, your "intolerance" betrays that you've forgotten that other people are capable of discovering, and doing, the good.

Homosexuals love to use this criteria to judge the people who condemn their actions. Anyone who suggests that homosexuality is wrong, not just for themselves but for everyone, is labeled as "intolerant" and dismissed as someone seeking to force their morality on others. "Live and let live," is the rallying cry in modern times—don't tell me how to behave in the privacy of my own bedroom, and I won't tell you how to behave either.

This attitude allows everyone the "freedom" to be selfish—as they should be—and theoretically keeps people from selfishly running over other people. But in reality it does nothing of the sort.

Dr. Seuss tells a story of the Zax, two creatures who are very bull-headed (or, as those of us with similar personalities like to say, "perseverant"). Their conflict began simply enough:

> One day, making tracks
> In the prairie of Prax,
> Came a North-Going Zax

And a South-Going Zax.
And it happened that both of them came to a
place
Where they bumped. There they stood.
Foot to foot. Face to face.[47]

Unfortunately, the conflict soon escalates, because both Zax are too—ahem—perseverant to step aside. The South-Going Zax eventually vows, "I'll stay here, not budging! I can and I will/If it makes you and me and the whole world stand still."[48] The North-Going Zax feels the same, and so their determination guarantees an impasse. The story ends in the only way it can:

Well . . .
Of course the world *didn't* stand still. The
world grew.
In a couple of years, the new highway came
through
And they built it right over those two stubborn
Zax
And left them there, standing un-budged in
their tracks.[49]

But the world *would* stand still if everyone in it had the same attitude as the Zax—and this is precisely the attitude that "absolute tolerance" fosters. Treating intolerance as the only deadly sin does not resolve ethical conflicts; it only ensures that people will become more unbudging in their moral dealings. Let me explain.

The proper response to the older woman who points out that you shouldn't have stolen her parking space because in so doing you imposed your morality on her, is to ask her not to impose her morality on you. She may believe that the parking space was rightfully hers; but after all, such a belief is only her belief, and it would be intolerant of her to expect you to abide by it. Likewise, we may say that Hitler did not have the right to kill Jews because he was imposing his moral beliefs on them, but he might readily respond that we should "tolerate" his moral beliefs instead of imposing ours on him. And so, like two Zax, Hitler and the world wind up foot to foot, face to face, with Hitler unwilling to allow the world to be intolerant of him, and the world unwilling to allow him to be intolerant of others' views.

In order for tolerance to work as an absolute, *it must be allowed not to tolerate certain actions* (like imposing your morality on others)—which is a paradox. Tolerance, if it is your only standard, must grow intolerant. This explains why homosexuals can justify their intolerance of the Christian worldview's intolerance of their lifestyle. Under this system, homosexuals can impose their absolute, tolerance, on Christians while failing to tolerate the Christian system of absolutes. This is the only way relativists can, if you'll pardon my Seuss, avoid the Zax stand-still effect.

Colson explains that the world lauds tolerance only in the sense that "everyone has a right to express his or her own views—as long as those views do not contain any suggestion of absolutes that would compete with the prevailing standard of relativism."[50] Relativists may tolerate everything except worldviews with absolutes—namely, Christianity and traditional Judaism. H.R. Rookmaaker puts it this way: "The revolutionaries speak of freedom, yet we find that if you are not for their kind of freedom, you have no right to say so."[51]

Worldly tolerance quickly grows intolerant.

This intolerance is often displayed prominently in science labs, especially when Christians voice their belief in the Genesis account of creation. Ken Ham, the director of Answers in Genesis (AIG), faced the full brunt of such intolerance when he announced his intention to build his new headquarters and a creation museum on 97 acres near Florence, Kentucky. His plans required a change in zoning, which was readily accepted by the zoning commission—and then the attacks began. One out-of-town lawyer voiced his opposition to the plan because creationists "are not scientists" and because "no reputable biologist believes in Creation." Other opponents characterized Ham as another Jim Jones, and falsely accused AIG of planning a militia compound and teaching followers that people who wear shorts are condemned to hell. By the time the onslaught of intolerance had passed, the fiscal court had denied Ham a hearing, and AIG was planning to relocate.[52]

How ironic. When we first noted that all non-Christians believe that man is basically good, it seemed like their worldviews contained lots of good news: we can trust our "inner voice,"[53] we can trust our fellow man, and we can work out our own salvation. Things seemed pretty cheery for the Frankenstein crowd. But as soon as we began to discuss putting all this into practice, we see why Pascal warned that "Man must not be allowed to believe that he is equal either to animals or to angels."[54] Now we find that non-Christians expect men to behave both pridefully and selfishly, and that most non-Christians don't have any absolute standard for their ethics. We find that selfishness leads only to pettiness, while Christianity encourages people to transcend themselves. Non-Christians give lip-service to tolerance, while remaining frankly intolerant of the Christian worldview. And in all this maze of ethical quandaries, it seems less and less likely that man will ever discover the way to work out his own salvation.

JUDGMENT DAY

Those in the Hyde crowd who recognize all of these quandaries might be tempted to feel proud of our own ethical accomplishments. We don't exalt selfishness and pride, and we understand that Christ calls us to a self-sacrificial love. We must be doing pretty well.

See how easy it is to forget that we're sinful? Christians must remember, everywhere and anytime, that *we're* not doing pretty well—we just have the opportunity to see God do good through us. This attitude of humility is best maintained if we remember, as Alexander Solzhenitsyn does, that Christians are no different than the cruelest prison guards, and are only distinguished from them by God's grace:

> And just so we don't go around flaunting too
> proudly the white mantle of the just, let
> everyone ask himself: 'If my life had turned out
> differently, might I myself not have become
> just such an executioner?'
> It is a dreadful question if one answers it
> honestly.[55]

Christians are sinners just like everyone is a sinner—the only difference is that Christians have been forgiven. As soon as we forget this, we will find ourselves falling back into our old patterns of pride and selfishness, considering ourselves better than others because we think we've got God on our side. This, too, is ironic—that the very people who are commanded to humble themselves and serve like Christ grow arrogant because He opened their eyes—but it happens all the time (just ask my wife). The temptation to be prideful is never far from the human heart; and our only respite is God.

Christians must bear in mind that, as Lewis says, "[T]he Author will have something to say to each of us on the part that each of us has played. The playing it well is what matters infinitely."[56] Christians will escape eternal damnation, but they will still face judgment on that fateful Day. Paul makes this clear in 1 Corinthians 3:12-15:

> If any man builds on this foundation [Jesus
> Christ] using gold, silver, costly stones, wood,
> hay or straw, his work will be shown for what it
> is, because the Day will bring it to light. It will
> be revealed with fire, and the fire will test the
> quality of each man's work. If what he has
> built survives, he will receive his reward. If it is
> burned up, he will suffer loss; he himself will
> be saved, but only as one escaping through the
> flames.

Christians are not absolved from right living just because they have been rescued from punishment. Rather, in the very act of rescuing us God makes it indisputably clear that He expects righteousness from us, by providing the perfect example of sacrifice, and by empowering us to live rightly by the indwelling of the Holy Spirit.

We are given all these things not so that we will grow haughty, but instead so that we will humble ourselves. In keeping with Lewis's analogy of God as Author, we shouldn't seek the lead role in His story, but instead should sacrifice ourselves and allow Him to use us however He chooses, no matter how trivial the role may seem:

> In *King Lear* (III:vii) there is a man who is such a minor character that Shakespeare has not given him even a name: he is merely 'First Servant.' All the characters around him—Regan, Cornwall, and Edmund—have fine long-term plans. They think they know how the story is going to end, and they are quite wrong. The servant has no such delusions. He has no notion how the play is going to go. But he understands the present scene. He sees an abomination (the blinding of old Gloucester) taking place. He will not stand it. His sword is out and pointed at his master's breast in a moment: then Regan stabs him dead from behind. That is his whole part: eight lines all told. But if it were real life and not a play, that is the part it would be best to have acted.[57]

How should Christians "act"? In the same way that our Savior acted, with humility. As He washed His disciples' feet, we too must learn to be selfless—to love. Though acting this way does not save us, it pleases our Creator and Redeemer. That should be enough.

In the meantime, non-Christians believe fervently that their salvation depends upon the way they behave. Man, according to this view, must begin as Franklin began this chapter, by practicing the virtue of selfishness. Taking this initial step allows man to move ahead with the real work of rescuing himself, which involves both improving himself and his environment. The next chapter will discuss some of the methods the Frankenstein crowd recommends to improve individuals, which necessarily entails a discussion of psychology. The chapter after that will discuss some of the methods the Frankenstein crowd recommends to improve society, which entails a discussion of government. Both discussions will render the gap between Hyde and Frankenstein wider and wider, as it becomes more evident that Christianity is radically different than every other worldview.

—And the difference is worth dying for, every day.

"And yet when I looked upon that ugly idol [Mr. Hyde] in the glass, I was conscious of no repugnance, rather of a leap of welcome. This, too, was myself. It seemed natural and human."[1]
—Dr. Jekyll

CHAPTER 4

SELF-HELPLESSNESS

U nlike many families, my family likes to discuss
religion and politics and everything we believe—and
we like these "discussions" to be loud. One of my
friends who had the misfortune to attend a family dinner
stared at the chaos for awhile and then shouted across the table
to me, "Who's listening?" It was a good question.

One of the most frequent catalysts for these family discussions is an aunt who, unfortunately, adheres to the New Age
worldview. Since she and I disagree on most every issue, it's
not hard to choose a topic and start a controversy. As we sort
through any given debate, we usually find that her position is
based on her faith in man, and my position is based on my
faith that man is inherently sinful. Since neither of us is
willing to concede that our faith may be wrong (we are both
dogmatic!), we end by agreeing to disagree.

During one discussion, however, I tried to throw my aunt a
change-up. Instead of baldly asserting that man was sinful, I
said, "You must think that Linda and I are the worst possible
parents, because we're going to tell our kids all the time that
they're sinful, and that they can't do anything good except by
God's power. We're going to teach them to deny their basic
goodness." Her response was adamant: she *did* consider us to
be good parents, and she was very pleased with the way we
were raising our children. Two weeks after this discussion, she

took the time to write us a letter apologizing for suggesting that we might be bad parents!

My aunt is too kind for her worldview. Though she responded honestly, she did not respond in a way that was consistent with her beliefs. As part of the Frankenstein crowd, she believes that my children can save themselves. The first step toward effecting this salvation, according to the New Age worldview and every other non-Christian worldview, is to recognize your inherent goodness—that is, to learn *self-esteem.* If my aunt really understood her faith, she would have to acknowledge that parents who teach their children that they are sinful are cruel people creating roadblocks in their children's path to salvation.

In order to save yourself, says the Frankenstein crowd, you must improve yourself. Depending on the specific worldview a non-Christian believes, this improvement is important either because it makes you acceptable to Allah, or because it allows you to transcend suffering, or because it hastens the evolutionary process, or for any other number of reasons. Regardless of the reason, this improvement cannot occur until a person recognizes that he is capable of improving himself—that he is basically good. Hence, we find non-Christians (at least those non-Christians who are consistent with their beliefs) promoting self-esteem. Men must know that they are good before they can unleash that goodness.

BELIEVING IN YOURSELF

The world is quick to blame low self-esteem for everything from acne to homicide. Neil Smelser claims that "many, if not most, of the major problems plaguing society have roots in the low self-esteem of many of the people who make up society."[2] Andrew Mecca agrees:

> The gathering of data and testimony at public hearings . . . built a consensus that a *primary* factor affecting how well or how poorly an individual functions in society is self-esteem. If this is the case, then, documenting this correlation and discovering effective means of promoting self-esteem might very well help to reduce the enormous cost in human suffering and the expenditure of billions in tax dollars caused by such problems as alcohol and drug abuse, crime, and child abuse.[3]

Shirley MacLaine thinks that this is true, and concludes that it is in the government's best interest to promote self-esteem: "If I ran the government I'd establish a cabinet post for self-esteem. Most of the problems in this country come from people who have absolutely no self-worth."[4]

MacLaine may not realize it, but her wish has been granted—at least in California. In 1986, state representative John Vasconcellos sponsored an initiative to create the California Task Force to Promote Self-Esteem. This Task Force sparked so much interest that each of the 58 counties in California jumped on the bandwagon and appointed a local self-esteem task force. Enthusiastic volunteers donated their time to this project because the drive to engender self-esteem fit their foundational *faith* that man is basically good. Vasconcellos, in the preface to a report entitled *The Social Importance of Self-Esteem*, says that there are only two options regarding the nature of man: people are either inherently sinful or basically good. He goes on to say that

> It is the latter vision—that human beings are innately inclined toward good and that free, healthy people become constructive and responsible—which underlies the philosophy and work of what has been called the 'self-esteem movement.' There is within this movement an implicit (and increasingly explicit) intuition, an assumption—a faith, if you will—that an essential and operational relationship exists between self-esteem and responsible human behavior, both personal and social. The term *self-esteem* implies a deeply felt appreciation of oneself and one's natural being, a trust of one's instincts and abilities.[5]

Operating according to the Frankenstein faith, it follows logically that one of the primary reasons that people do bad things is because they don't esteem themselves enough to trust their inner goodness. Not surprisingly, the California Task Force reached just such a conclusion in their *Final Report*: "Through all of our studies and research, we of the Task Force have become convinced that self-esteem is central to most of the personal and social problems that plague human life in today's world."[6] In other words, if every person could learn to trust his or her basically good impulses, we could save ourselves *and* eradicate most of the world's problems.

If this is true, then it's never too early to begin teaching people self-esteem—especially when you consider how much damage certain families and churches might have already inflicted by teaching children that they are sinful.[7] Members of the Frankenstein crowd must saturate the schools with self-esteem programs. Many of these programs are pretty watered down, but instances of extremism are easy to find: in the Halsey Schools, the word *bad* is forbidden—you can't say it—and every student gets an award every year, regardless of their level of achievement (in fact, the schools hold an award ceremony every six weeks). Kindergarten children in these schools, according to an article in *Newsweek*, "learn to count by being handed pictures of objects and *told how many there are instead of figuring it out themselves.*"[8] (Apparently the italics indicate that even the *Newsweek* reporter was shocked by this.) In Tennessee, students are asked to rank their self-esteem on a Self-Concept Scale that includes statements like, "I am satisfied with my moral behavior"—a statement that clearly implies that the individual is the yardstick for measuring morality.

The point of all these exercises? To help children feel better about themselves, so they can go about the business of saving themselves. Self-esteem, for the Frankenstein crowd, is the first step toward salvation.

But even if a person learns self-esteem, the road to salvation is not always clear. As a person seeks to follow his trustworthy inner impulses, he may often find his road blocked by two formidable barriers: *guilt* and *suffering*. Both of these barriers can prevent a man from rescuing himself.

GUILT AND SUFFERING

Guilt is especially problematic for the non-Christian because, technically speaking, a person is never guilty. Most non-Christians would admit that men occasionally behave badly—but only the *behavior* is bad, not the man. In other words, a Muslim would certainly say that a man who kills someone is "guilty" of murder and deserving of punishment, but he could not say that the act of murder resulted from the man being "guilty" of a corrupt, sinful nature. The Frankenstein crowd often condemns behavior, but they should never condemn the man—because the man is basically good. Thus, a person may feel guilty about some of the things he has done, but he should never feel guilty about who he fundamentally is. Only the Christian says that man is guilty just by virtue of being born a descendant of Adam.

Much to the non-Christian's surprise, however, people often feel guilty even though the world would describe their attitudes and actions as "normal" or "justifiable." Men and women who have been told to trust their inner voices often find themselves regretting that trust, feeling guilty about what their natural self has caused them to do or say. This in turn may lead people to distrust their inner voice, and thus lose their guide on their road to salvation. If the non-Christian is to achieve salvation, he must eradicate guilt feelings.

He must also dodge suffering. Pain and mental anguish, depending on the non-Christian's worldview, are either meaningless or warning signs. The atheist chooses the former explanation, believing that all life arose by chance and therefore that existence is purposeless. As biologist Stephen Jay Gould explains, "If humanity arose just yesterday [comparatively speaking, assuming that the earth is more than four billion years old] as a small twig on one branch of a flourishing tree, then life may not, in any genuine sense, exist for us or because of us. Perhaps we are only an afterthought, a kind of cosmic accident, just one bauble on the Christmas tree of evolution."[9] As baubles, of course, we can hardly expect our cracks and dents to signify anything. They just happen, like all suffering happens. And if suffering is meaningless, why experience it? It just gets in the way of feeling good about ourselves.

Most other non-Christian worldviews view suffering as a warning sign. According to traditional Judaism, Buddhism, the New Age, Islam, Hinduism and various pseudo-Christian cults, suffering happens only when we get off-track. Once we place ourselves back on the road to salvation, the suffering will disappear. Consider:

For the traditional Jew, suffering occurs when he distances himself from God. According to the Old Testament, God promised to bless the Jews if they obey Him, and so any suffering must result from the Jew breaking his end of the bargain. According to this worldview, suffering is a sign that God expects more righteousness from His follower, which in turn is a warning that the Jew is in jeopardy of failing to rescue himself. Muslims, Mormons and Jehovah's Witnesses, if they are consistent with their worldviews, believe similar versions of this basic pattern—when their actions displease their god, the god warns them by causing them to suffer. For the Buddhist, salvation (i.e., nirvana) occurs when we learn to view all suffering as illusory—thus, when we experience suffering it's a good indication that we have wandered from the Noble Eightfold Path. For the Hindu, suffering is punishment for bad karma—which indicates that he had better work harder to develop good karma in this life. And for the New Age adherent . . .

As it happens, New Age author Marianne Williamson provides us with a terrific example of the New Age attitude toward suffering. Williamson offers seminars to help AIDS patients deal with their disease, and her approach is, to put it mildly, unique. She begins by telling seminar participants that they must stop thinking of AIDS as Acquired Immune Deficiency Syndrome and instead think of it as "Angels-In-Darth Vader-Suits."[10] According to Williamson, the reason people suffer is because they have not learned to "respond to the problem with love instead of fear."[11] If we can respond to our suffering in love, the suffering will heal. She explains it like this:

> When a child presents a cut finger to his or her mother, the woman doesn't say, "Bad cut." Rather, she kisses the finger, showers it with love in an unconscious, instinctive activation of the healing process. Why should we think differently about critical illness? Cancer and AIDS and other serious illnesses are physical manifestations of a psychic scream, and their message is not "Hate me," but "Love me."[12]

Like the mother kissing the boo-boo, AIDS patients should kiss their AIDS—that is, they must embrace the cause of their suffering.

And things get stranger. Williamson encourages the seminar participants to use a visualization in which they "Imagine the AIDS virus as Darth Vader, and then unzip his suit to allow an angel to emerge"[13] (hence her use of the term *Angels-In-DarthVader Suits*). Supposedly, visualizing this angel makes it easier for participants to love their AIDS, as does another exercise she recommends: writing a love letter to the

AIDS virus! In her best-selling book *A Return to Love*, Williamson reprints some of these letters, which contain statements like: "Dear AIDS . . . I'm a grown-up thanks to your appearance in my life. You've given me a reason to live and I love you for it."[14] And just when you thought it couldn't possibly get any stranger, Williamson asks seminar participants to write a love letter *back* to themselves, from their AIDS!! One participant imagined his AIDS virus writing, "Please don't hate me and try to destroy me. Love me. Let's talk and listen to each other and try to live in peace."[15]

We'll discuss the cruelty inherent in this perspective later in this chapter. For now, it is enough to recognize that believing in the New Age worldview necessitates the conclusion that *suffering is your own fault*. If a person suffers from a disease instead of converting the disease into a positive energy in his life, it's his fault for not responding properly to the disease.[16] Put simply, if a person is in touch with his godhood, bad things won't happen to him. Suffering only results from forgetting that we are god. Shakti Gawain says bluntly, "Every time you don't trust yourself and don't follow your inner truth, you decrease your aliveness and your body will reflect this with a loss of vitality, numbness, pain, and eventually, physical disease."[17] Other New Age leaders suggest that our inability to get in touch with our godhood may be manifested through poverty, or a rotten job, or broken relationships.

All of the other "warning sign" worldviews must also conclude that suffering is our own fault. If the only purpose of suffering is to warn us when we get off-track, then we may consistently avoid suffering by always behaving properly and therefore escaping the need for correction. If the Jew or Muslim would only work harder at obedience, or the Buddhist would only work harder at following the Noble Eightfold Path, they need never suffer. If any bad thing happens to them, it happened precisely because they weren't good enough.

Suffering, for the non-Christian, is best avoided. And guilt should not exist. Clearly, non-Christians must find a way to cope with both these problems. Where should they turn? To many, it seems logical to turn to psychology.

THE ALLURE OF PSYCHOLOGY

Psychology is, after all, a profession dedicated to helping people achieve mental well-being. Psychologists seek to minimize mental and emotional anguish, and since both guilt and suffering cause this anguish, it seems reasonable to expect psychology to demolish these roadblocks. Many secular psychologists encourage this conclusion, leading people to believe (as they once caused William Kilpatrick to believe) that "suffering was not the common lot of humanity but some kind of foolish mistake that could be avoided by a better understanding of human dynamics."[18] If this is true, non-Christians would be foolish *not* to rely on secular psychology.

Accordingly, the twentieth century has produced a bumper crop of people lying on couches anxiously contemplating their dreams, their fears, their relationship with their mothers, their self-actualization, and their inner child. In the name of psychology people wear nothing but giant diapers and lunge about in a giant playpen (a version of primal scream therapy), or allow themselves to be hypnotized to dredge up allegedly repressed memories. People spend thousands of dollars and literally walk across hot coals.

They take these risks because the potential reward is tremendous: they might learn to trust their basic goodness, rid themselves of guilt feelings, and avoid almost all physical and emotional anguish. And if they can manage all this, it's safe to assume that they are well on their way to working out their own salvation. Secular psychology is so alluring to moderns because it might have the power to break down all the barriers on the road to redemption.

Which brings us to a good question: How can we know if secular psychology is working? What results would we expect in the lives of people who have relied on worldly psychology to help them achieve mental health?

One quite obvious result we would expect is to see people with specific mental illnesses recovering from those illnesses. But for people without quantifiable illnesses, the only indication that mainstream psychology is helping would be that they are feeling better about themselves; avoiding suffering and guilt should make them happier. It seems reasonable to expect that happiness would be one of the by-products of successful secular psychology.

If man is good, then he must simply listen to, and obey, his basic goodness in order to save himself. As man moves closer to nirvana, or utopia, or exaltation, or whatever perfection he expects to attain, he should find himself more "blessed" or more enlightened and therefore happier. Williamson makes this clear: "God's will is that we be happy now."[19] And elsewhere she says,

> Heaven . . . is not something we'll experience "later." "Later" is just a thought. "Be of good cheer," said Jesus "for I have overcome the

world." He realized, and so can we all, that the
world has no power before the power of God.
It is not real. It is only an illusion. God has
created love as the only reality, the only power.
And so it is.[20]

Not every member of the Frankenstein crowd would put it this
way, of course, but most would expect fundamentally the same
thing. If we're in touch with our goodness, good things should
follow—whether those good things be blessings from God or
simply the direct result of our own hard work.

In the real world, however, people who don't know Christ
seldom find themselves truly happy. "A trillion experiments,"
says Peter Kreeft, "have proved one point over and over past all
doubt: That whenever we aim at happiness as if we were God,
by exerting our power and control, we end up in unhappiness,
whether we get the thing we wanted or not."[21] This makes
sense, if Christianity is true: how could a being created to
glorify God feel happy living separate from God and living
only to glorify himself? A person may aim at other things
besides God for a time, and occasionally feel happy in the
"thrill of the chase," but this happiness cannot last.

Psychology can't change that fact, no matter how many
psychologists imply that it can. What's more, psychology can't
remove all guilt or alleviate most suffering or even cause people
to feel good about themselves. About all that secular psychology can accomplish is to encourage people to be selfish,
something that everyone already knows how to do quite well.

Secular psychologists should not feel bad about their
failures, however—because they are attempting the impossible.
No theory and no therapy can get rid of guilt or suffering, or

make unredeemed man feel good about himself. These things can't happen, because man is not basically good. Secular psychologists lose touch with reality at the same point all non-Christians lose touch with reality: they believe in the wrong monster. They misunderstand the nature of man.

Unfortunately, Christian psychology often fails as miserably as secular psychology, because too many Christians think that "Christian psychology" is simply a matter of studying Sigmund Freud, Carl Jung, and Carl Rogers and keeping a Bible on your desk. Too many Christians try to blend secular psychological concepts with the Christian worldview, forgetting that these elements *must* be incompatible because the former are based on man's inherent goodness and the latter is based on man's inherent sinfulness. To put it bluntly, too many Christians think that the best counselor is the man with the most education in the field of psychology, which overlooks the fact that virtually all of this education is based on the completely false assumption that man is basically good. From Freud to Jung to Rogers, from B.F. Skinner to Abraham Maslow to Erich Fromm to M. Scott Peck, virtually every "founding father" psychologist belongs to the Frankenstein crowd. As Kilpatrick notes, "[P]sychological theory doesn't take account of the Fall; it takes the position that there are no bad natural inclinations."[22] Why, then, would Christians expect someone steeped in these theories to have any insight at all regarding how men should think or act?

The best psychology—and the only proper "Christian psychology"—rejects all theories based on the assumption that man is basically good, and instead builds a theory of counseling based on the biblical account of the Fall. Most Christians who have done this, including Jay Adams and Kilpatrick, shy away from the term "psychology" altogether, because the word itself is overburdened with the baggage of Frankenstein. I like the way Kilpatrick puts it: "In short, although Christianity is more than a psychology, it happens to be better psychology than psychology is."[23] He describes psychology and Christianity as "competing faiths. If you seriously hold to one set of values, you will logically have to reject the other."[24]

Tragically, many Christians ignore this warning and try to blend their faith with the world's faith in psychology. The tragedy is two-fold: these Christians misrepresent biblical doctrine, and then, because they tie themselves to psychological concepts that are out of touch with reality, they fail to help their patients. To avoid such mistakes, Christians should instead recognize the flaws inherent in modern psychology and seek to understand the biblical perspective on self-esteem, guilt and suffering.

The shortcomings of secular psychology are fairly obvious. Some of the founding fathers of psychology eventually recognized these flaws themselves, and recanted some of their earlier theories. Maslow asked the question late in life, "Who should teach whom? Youngsters teach the elders or vice versa? It got me in a conflict about my education theory."[25] He eventually concluded that children could not achieve self-actualization, which seems to contradict his previous assumption that man is basically good. Likewise, one of Rogers' co-workers, William Coulson, eventually grew disenchanted with Rogers' psychological models, and spoke out against the continued implementation of these models in public schools. Freud dramatically underscored psychology's inability to help people when, after a lifetime of seeking to improve men, he sneered, "I have found little that is 'good' about human beings on the whole. In my experience most of them are trash . . ."[26]

But the greatest indication of the shortcomings of modern psychology is empirical evidence. Kilpatrick provides a brief survey of some recent studies:

> The first indication that psychology must be ineffective came in 1952 when Hans Eysenck of the Institute of Psychiatry, University of London, discovered that neurotic people who do not receive therapy are as likely to recover as those who do. Psychotherapy, he found, was not any more effective than the simple passage of time. Additional studies by other researchers showed similar results. Then Dr. Eugene Levitt of the Indiana University School of Medicine found that disturbed children who were not treated recovered at the same rate as disturbed children who were. A further indication of the problem was revealed in the results of the extensive Cambridge-Somerville Youth Study. The researchers found that uncounseled juvenile delinquents had a lower rate of further trouble than counseled ones. Other studies have shown that untrained lay people do as well as psychiatrists or clinical psychologists in treating patients. And the Rosenham studies indicated that mental hospital staff could not even tell normal people from genuinely disturbed ones. It is possible to go on with the list. It is quite a long one. But

I hope this is sufficient to make the point that
when psychologists rush in to help, they are
not particularly successful.[27]

They are not successful because they, like all non-Christians,
misunderstand the nature of man and therefore misunderstand
self-esteem, guilt, and suffering. Examining the biblical view
of these "psychological" concepts will reveal just how badly
modern psychology misses the mark.

THE BIBLE AND SELF-ESTEEM

As grinch-like as it seems, the Bible does not promote self-
esteem, at least in the worldly sense of the word. Though
many Christians like to point to the second greatest commandment, "Love your neighbor as yourself" and conclude that we
must learn to love ourselves before we can love God or our
neighbor, such a conclusion is unbiblical. Rather, we should
recognize that the second greatest commandment *presupposes*
men loving themselves, treating it as self-evident that every
man begins by esteeming himself. The very condition of
fallenness implies a focus on self rather than on God—a desire
to fulfill ourselves rather than our duties to our Creator.
Remember Philippians 2:3? "Do nothing out of selfish ambition or vain conceit, but in humility consider others better
than yourselves." Such a command flaunts the worldly concept of self-esteem, and explains instead that we need to think
less of ourselves and more of our fellow man!

Many Christians, however, think that compassion requires
them to promote self-esteem. Kilpatrick speaks of a priest he
knows who claimed that the purpose of Christ's coming was to

say, "You're O.K. and I'm O.K." Elsewhere he describes a
youth Bible study that contains the question: "Do you think
Moses had a good image or a bad image of himself?"[28] Other
Christians, though perhaps not as enamored with self-esteem
as this priest or this Bible study, still talk like self-esteem is a
viable concept, especially when you consider extreme cases like
the person contemplating suicide. These Christians diagnose
such a person as suffering from low self-esteem, and recommend that they learn to value themselves. But a moment's
reflection reveals that the suicidal person's self-esteem is not too
low, but too high: he considers his own personal happiness to
be more important than His Creator's purpose for His life, and
he is unconcerned about the emotional trauma that his death
will inflict on those close to him. The person contemplating
suicide does indeed need counseling, but the counseling should
be directly concerned with teaching him to think less of
himself and more of God.

Though the Christian rejection of the concept of self-
esteem may seem callous, it is actually more merciful than the
psychologist's desire to teach people self-esteem. Men, in order
to be redeemed, do not need to love themselves more and thus
get in touch with their inner goodness; rather, they need to
respond like Job responded to God's holiness: "I despise myself
and repent in dust and ashes" (Job 42:6). As C.S. Lewis warns,
"Mercy, detached from Justice, grows unmerciful."[29] The self-
esteem movement seeks to be merciful toward people, but in
reality it *unmercifully* draws them into themselves and away
from God. If the Bible is true, the best thing a person can do
is not affirm himself, but instead deny himself and follow
Christ. Adams says bluntly,

The proper thing to encourage, according to
the Word of God, is self-denial. The command to deny self occurs six times explicitly in
the Gospels, but the concept is everywhere in
Scripture. That is what the Lord was getting at
when He told His disciples to forget their own
interests and put His affairs first ('seek first the
kingdom of God and His righteousness').[30]

Please notice that this self-denial is *not* the same thing as self-
hatred. The Christian rejection of self-esteem is a rejection of
focus on self, not a rejection of self. Once our focus shifts to
God, we may recognize the value with which God has endowed us by virtue of creating us in His own image and loving
us. Lewis writes, "We are, not metaphorically but in very
truth, a Divine work of art, something that God is making,
and therefore something with which He will not be satisfied
until it has a certain character."[31] Man has no merits on his
own, but by the grace of God he can be shaped into a "Divine
work of art." We can begin this process by humbling ourselves
and esteeming God.

Events in the real world support the belief that the self-
esteem movement is, at the very least, misguided. Although
MacLaine and many others suggest that there are lots of people
who suffer from low self-esteem, a recent study indicates just
the opposite:

In 'leadership ability,' 70 percent [of American
high school students surveyed] rated themselves above average, 2 percent below average.
Sixty percent view themselves as better than

average in 'athletic ability,' and only 6 percent
as below average. In 'ability to get along with
others,' zero percent of the 829,000 students
who responded rated themselves below average,
60 percent rated themselves in the top 10
percent, and 25 percent see themselves among
the top 1 percent.[32]

Significantly, most Americans don't believe they suffer from
low self-esteem, but they think they know a lot of people who
do: "Although only one in 10 Americans believes he personally
suffers from low self-esteem, according to a *Newsweek* Gallup
Poll, more than 50 percent diagnose the condition in someone
else in their families."[33] Low self-esteem is the witch-hunt of
the twentieth century: though I may not be a witch, I have
quite a few neighbors who are.

With all these Americans feeling good about themselves,
non-Christians should expect that our high self-esteem will
translate into better performance. But a study by Harold
Stevenson bursts that bubble, as *Newsweek* explains: "American
schoolchildren rank far ahead of students in Japan, Taiwan and
China in self-confidence about their abilities in math. Unfortunately, this achievement was marred by the fact that
Americans were far behind in *actual performance* in math."[34] In
fact, the only area that self-esteem seems to impact is a little
embarrassing for the self-esteem movement: "[T]wo studies
linked *high* self-esteem with increased sexual activity by
teens"![35]

Despite all the optimism of the California Task Force to
Promote Self-Esteem, data suggests that Americans have plenty
of self-esteem and yet still behave badly (perhaps even worse

than the way they behaved prior to the self-esteem movement). Smelser grudgingly confesses this in one of the reports published by the task force: "One of the disappointing aspects of every chapter in this volume . . . is how low the associations between self-esteem and its consequences are in research to date."[36] Quite simply, the self-esteem movement has succeeded in promoting self-esteem, but none of the benefits of high self-esteem have resulted. We like ourselves, but we continue to behave badly.

THE BIBLE AND GUILT

It seems logical to ask here, as Kilpatrick asks, "Are we . . . to like ourselves regardless of how we behave?"[37] According to the Frankenstein crowd, we should. Guilt, remember, is only something that slows down our efforts to save ourselves. People may occasionally be guilty of bad actions, but people themselves cannot be bad. In order to trust our inner goodness, we must never feel so guilty that we begin to distrust ourselves. Thus, the secular psychologist often encourages his patients to stop feeling guilty.

The story of Jekyll and Hyde reminds us that such advice is impossible to obey. Just as Jekyll feels more and more guilty about Hyde, another character reveals that he, too, has his own shortcomings. We are told that the lawyer Utterson, when called upon to reflect on his own life, feels guilt: "His past was fairly blameless; few men could read the rolls of their life with less apprehension; yet he was humbled to the dust by the many ill things he had done . . ."[38] Even the "best" men, according to Stevenson, have a Hyde that makes them guilty.

Telling a non-Christian to stop feeling guilty is like telling him to stop feeling. God in His graciousness has provided us with a conscience that informs us of our guilt (Romans 2:14-15). Guilt feelings are a good thing. People who have not been rescued by Christ's work on the cross *should* feel guilty, because they are sinful beings in rebellion against their righteous Creator. This sense of guilt helps drive them to seek answers outside of themselves, and by the power of the Holy Spirit encourages them to rely on Christ to remove their guilt.

Nor are non-Christians the only ones who should feel guilt. When Christians break God's laws, they should recognize that they are guilty of displeasing God. The difference between Christian guilt and non-Christian guilt, however, is immense: Christians know that their guilt has been removed by Christ's work on the cross, and so our guilt need not overwhelm us. Christians may repent and move on. Non-Christians, on the other hand, are stuck with a guilt that they are told they should not feel, and yet cannot remove no matter how hard they try.

The non-Christian attitude toward guilt *seems* like a comfortable attitude that frees men from anxiety and concern, but in reality it traps them on an "effort treadmill." Whenever they feel guilty, they should feel guilty for feeling guilty, and work harder to eradicate that guilt. Hamsters running furiously inside a wheel have a better chance of reaching their destination than do sinful men seeking to erase their guilt before God.

Ironically, although modern psychology seeks to help people avoid all guilt, it actually *increases* their burden. "[W]hen you have nothing and no one to rely on but yourself," writes Kilpatrick, "life becomes very serious indeed. If, in addition, the self is made out by all the experts to be some sort of holy wonder machine, and if you have not yet found the switch, your burden is that much more."[39] Life becomes deadly serious for the man who must work out his own salvation; only the Christian may find rest and comfort in relying on a Redeemer. Christians proclaim with Blaise Pascal, "Be comforted; it is not from yourself that you must expect it, but on the contrary you must expect it by expecting nothing from yourself."[40]

Again we discover that the bad news that man is sinful leads us to really good news. Kilpatrick explains:

> That is why G.K. Chesterton could say that the doctrine of original sin was the most cheerful idea he knew of. If one takes the Christian view and accepts sin, failure, and shortcoming as the common lot of a fallen race rather than a personal inadequacy, the burden of guilt becomes more bearable and understandable.[41]

And when one accepts Christ as his or her Savior, one may transfer the burden of guilt to Him on the cross, and be free indeed.

The Christian view of guilt is not as simplistic as the worldly view, but it is infinitely more comforting. Guilt is real, but it can be removed by Christ's work on the cross. Both Christians and non-Christians should feel guilty when they behave badly, but Christians may repent and see Christ remove their burden. Not all guilt feelings are really deserved, of course, but the guilt that *is* justified points us to our Savior and therefore should not be ignored. Francis Schaeffer explains this distinction: "Psychological guilt is actual and cruel. But Christians know that there is also real guilt, moral guilt before a holy God. It is not a matter only of psychological guilt; that is the distinction."[42] The world treats all guilt as psychological—that is, phantom—guilt. But Christians understand that man is sinful and therefore truly guilty before his Creator. Nothing we do, and nothing psychologists do, can remove this guilt—only Christ can.

THE BIBLE AND SUFFERING

Christians further distinguish themselves from the world by responding differently to suffering. Just as Christians believe that not all guilt should be ignored, we believe that not all suffering should be avoided. While the world says that suffering is either meaningless or our own fault, Christians respond that suffering is meaningful and may or may not be our own fault.

Kilpatrick believes that this difference between the Christian response to suffering and the worldly response is the most significant criteria for determining which worldview is true: "The real test of a theory or way of life, however, is not whether it can relieve pain but what it says about the pain it cannot relieve. And this is where, I believe, psychology lets us down and Christianity supports us . . ."[43]

Suppose for a moment that you are blind, and that science can do nothing to restore your vision. The atheist must respond by saying that you simply have bad luck, and that it's really a shame that you're blind because you can't expect anything good to come from it. "The bulk of the world's pain," says Kilpatrick, "is written off as a bad expense."[44] Any other non-Christian must say that your inability to see is really your own fault (or perhaps your parents' fault, as Jesus' disciples suggest in John 9:2, in keeping with the Jewish worldview) or else deny that you are actually suffering. The Hindu blames bad karma, the Muslim blames a failure to obey, the New Age proponent blames your failure to get in touch with your godhood and create the proper reality, the Buddhist says that suffering is illusory, etc.

None of these responses provide any comfort for the blind man—in fact, they add to his mental anguish by rendering his suffering meaningless or, worse still, a result of his own failings. This is callous at best, and—if Christianity is true—downright cruel. Dorothy Sayers explains:

> [H]ere Christianity has its enormous advantage over every other religion in the world. It is the *only* religion that gives value to evil and suffering. It affirms—not, like Christian Science, that evil has no real existence, nor yet, like Buddhism, that good consists in a refusal to experience evil—but that perfection is attained through the active and positive effort to wrench a real good out of a real evil.[45]

The Christian attitude toward suffering is best summarized by Joseph as he forgives his brothers. Many people tend to picture Joseph only as the conquering hero who rescued many people from starvation during his tenure in the Egyptian government, but that overlooks the fact that Joseph suffered a great deal throughout his life. His brothers hated him—so much, in fact, that they wanted to kill him. He found himself thrown into a pit by those closest to him, and then sold into slavery. He was taken away from his family to a foreign land where he did not know a single person. When he eventually was trusted by people in Egypt, he was falsely accused by Potiphar's wife and thrown into prison. The friends that he meets in prison promise to try to help him, and then forget all about him when they are released. Throughout his life he suffers hatred, rejection, loneliness, betrayal and (it is safe to assume) despair. And yet Joseph did not view his suffering as meaningless or something he should have avoided, but instead as a part of God's perfect plan. When his brothers finally groveled before him after he saved them from starvation, Joseph explained the biblical view of suffering: "You intended to harm me, but God intended it for good to accomplish what is now being done, the saving of many lives" (Genesis 50:20). Though men or Satan may make bad things happen, God can use even those bad circumstances for good.

Non-Christians love to use the "problem of evil" to embarrass Christians. They often ask us why, if God is both holy and all-powerful, bad things happen. But evil is really the world's problem. If the God of the Bible does not exist, what can the world say to the suffering individual? But if God exists, man may find profound comfort in the knowledge that He is in control and is bringing all of history together toward His appointed end! The horrible suffering of Christ on the cross brought about more good than if suffering had never been brought into existence by the rebellion of men and angels, thanks to the grace of God. Without this grace, what reason can any man find to endure suffering?

What could be more cruel than telling AIDS patients that they can heal themselves by responding to their disease in love, when in fact they can no more rid themselves of their disease than they can jump over Pikes Peak? What could be more unkind than to tell a blind man that his suffering is illusion? And yet such responses are the only responses that the non-Christian can offer. Precisely at the point where men most need hope, the world deals only in false hope and denial.

Christianity offers real hope. My favorite verse in the Bible is the verse twisted by Williamson earlier in this chapter, John 16:33. Christ promises that "In this world you will have trouble, but take heart! I have overcome the world." To properly understand suffering, we must understand both guarantees contained in this promise. First the good news: Christ is in control! He has vanquished the world and been granted all authority in heaven and earth (Matthew 28:18), and He brings all things together for good. Christians, as Lewis says, know the end of the story—and it's a happy ending. Someday all our suffering on earth will seem like a distant dream, and reality will be the most joyous wedding feast imaginable.

But this does not mean that Christians who suffer today don't really experience anguish. In this world, suffering is real and painful. Just like everyone else, Christians who suffer often wish, in their darkest times, that their suffering could be avoided. Christianity does not lessen the pain or cause Christians to skip through life like silly Barney dolls. If we are to properly understand reality, we must remember the first half of Christ's guarantee: in this world we will face trouble. Not maybe. Not possibly. A basic fact: every man and woman suffers. The world is not an illusion, and we can expect to experience real pain while we're here.

Above all things, the Christian attitude toward suffering is not glib. We must never behave as though suffering isn't a big deal, or as though good Christians don't suffer. Everyone suffers, and it hurts. The difference between Christianity and all other worldviews is not that Christianity can remove suffering, but that Christianity can give meaning to suffering. Our suffering won't be any easier, but it will be more bearable, if we remember that God can use bad things for good. Suffering hurts either way, but as Kilpatrick explains, "Dumb, meaningless suffering is harder to take than suffering that seems to have a purpose."[46]

By acknowledging that suffering happens to everyone, as Christ explained, we can prepare ourselves for bad times. Once we accept the fact that anguish is the lot of every person, when we experience pain we won't shake our fists at God as though He singled us out. Instead of lashing out blindly when we're hurt, Christians may cast about for the good that God can manifest through suffering. Again, this doesn't mean that we paint a phony smile on our face wherever we go; it just means that we recognize God's omnipotence. Remember Joseph; he didn't act like bad things hadn't happened—but he also wisely sought to understand how God could work through those bad circumstances. As Christians grow into the spiritual maturity of Joseph, we may begin to experience the mysterious mindset described in James 1:2-3: "Consider it pure joy, my brothers, whenever you face trials of many kinds, because you know that the testing of your faith develops perseverance." No Christian will ever like suffering, but by God's grace we may begin to experience a "peace that passes all understanding" as we seek His purpose in pain.

Suffering is especially hard on non-Christians because they think that the purpose of life is to grow happier and happier as they move toward salvation.[47] Christians, on the other hand, should recognize that our purpose is to follow Christ, and that following Him will cause us a lot of hardship until we reach our destination. Whittaker Chambers understands this: "I did not suppose that those words, 'All will be well with you,' implied my happiness, for I never supposed that what man means by well-being and what well-being means to God could possibly be the same. They might be as different as joy and suffering."[48] In this world the Christian must expect that suffering will often overwhelm happiness, but he must also expect that *when we look back on our lives it will all be worth it.* Dietrich Bonhoeffer, a Christian who suffered and died in a Nazi prison camp, writes, "After he has been following Christ for a long time, the disciple of Jesus will be asked 'Lacked ye anything?' and he will answer 'Nothing, Lord.' How could he when he knows that despite hunger and nakedness, persecution and danger, the Lord is always at his side?"[49] Sayers acknowledges the bad news by admitting that man "cannot be good and cannot be happy," but she continues with the good news: "there are certain eternal achievements that make even happiness look like trash."[50] On the Day of Judgment, God will not ask us if we were happy; He will ask us if we followed Him. On that day we will boast, as Paul boasted, of our stripes and our bruises.

This does not mean, of course, that Christians should never avoid suffering. When you knock off the liquor store and suffer 20 years in prison, it's safe to say that you should have avoided knocking off the liquor store and thereby avoided imprisonment. Some suffering really is our own fault—that is, it results directly from bad choices on our part—and nobody (least of all God) demands that you make bad choices just so you can experience suffering.

But suffering also results from *good* choices. The Christian who obeys God and sacrifices himself will often suffer as a result of that decision. Kilpatrick distinguishes between suffering that results from bad choices and suffering that results from good choices:

> Although some of our problems come from stupidity or selfishness on our part, many come because we have tried to do something worthwhile such as create a family and provide for it. Most of us struggle and sacrifice for people or causes outside ourselves, and sometimes even at the cost of our self-interest. We may risk suffering for the sake of a child, for the sake of a parent, even for God's sake.[51]

By deciding to die to ourselves, Christians ensure that they will suffer for the sake of others. Paradoxically, this suffering will also prove to be for our own sake—because God can use it to make us "mature and complete, not lacking anything" (James 1:4). Suffering, for the Christian, has meaning both for ourselves and for others.

Viktor Frankl, a psychologist who endured a hundred lifetimes' worth of suffering at Auschwitz and other Nazi camps, concluded from his experience that "If there is a meaning in life at all, then there must be a meaning in suffering."[52] The only meaning any non-Christian worldview can attach to suffering is that it is your own fault. Christianity, on the other hand, infuses *all* suffering with meaning.

Frankl comes very close to recognizing the truth of Christianity, but unfortunately falls short. He decided that the reason some people survived prison camp and others didn't was because some people could find a meaning in suffering, and others could not. This seems reasonable; but Frankl goes on to say that many things can give a man's life—and consequently his suffering—meaning, from writing a book to caring for a family. This misses the mark. While it's true that we may endure suffering for the sake of our family, the suffering itself is not of any value *unless* God in His power purifies us in its flames. Man cannot endow suffering with value, because man is not the source of goodness. We must look to that Source to find the real meaning in suffering.

Frankl never quite understands this, but he understands a great deal more about suffering than most non-Christians. Even though he is a psychologist who admired Freud, he ultimately rejects the psychological mindset that pursues self-esteem and seeks to eradicate all guilt and suffering, and calls for people to worry less about themselves and more about others. He recognizes that the men who responded properly to suffering in prison camps acted selflessly: "We who lived in concentration camps can remember the men who walked through the huts comforting others, giving away their last piece of bread."[53] Memories like this caused him to reject selfishness: "Human existence is essentially self-transcendence rather than self-actualization,"[54] and to call every man to get off the analyst's couch and to "stop asking about the meaning of life, and instead to think of ourselves as those who [are] being questioned by life—daily and hourly. Our answer must consist, not in talk and meditation, but in right action and right conduct."[55]

Auschwitz revealed to Frankl, once and for all, the bankruptcy of modern psychological theory and the need for a worldview that infused suffering with meaning. Christians should be the first to agree: the worldly, psychological attitude toward self-esteem, guilt and suffering is unacceptable. The best psychology is not getting in touch with your inner goodness or disowning guilt feelings, but following Christ.

Mental health is not about realizing you are basically good; instead, it depends upon the realization that Christ died for your sins and loves you deeply. Certain mental illnesses are physical and require medical treatment, but most mental distress comes from misunderstanding who man is and who God is. As Schaeffer says, "The basic psychological problem is trying to be what we are not, and trying to carry what we cannot carry. Most of all, the basic problem is not being willing to be the creatures we are before the Creator."[56] The road to mental health begins with acknowledging our sinfulness and relying on Christ to wash away that sin and redeem us.

After this, we must recognize Christ's call to follow Him, and reject the virtue of selfishness. Dying to self frees us from "the tyranny of self" and affords us a better perspective on reality, which in turn allows us to take ourselves a little less seriously. "The man who makes faces to amuse a baby," writes Kilpatrick, "gives up his dignity; so does the man who roars with laughter. The essential condition for having fun is to forget your dignity, that is, to forget yourself."[57] And elsewhere he says, "The best times are those high moments of self-loss, moments when, immersed in talk or lost in laughter, we are more ourselves than ever."[58]

Secular psychology actually encourages mental illness by encouraging selfishness. "Extreme forms of mental illness," says Kilpatrick, "are always extreme cases of self-absorption. . . . The distinctive quality, the thing that literally sets paranoid people apart, is hyper-self-consciousness."[59] If man really is basically good, it would be a good thing for him to turn his eyes inward, but because man is sinful, he must look outside himself for answers. Relying on himself only increases his anxiety and distress.

By relying on Christ and following Him, Christians see their guilt erased and their suffering infused with meaning. Christians will still face times of mental and emotional distress, but when they do they may be comforted by the knowledge that they are saved by grace rather than their own efforts. We need not be perfect, though God is moving us toward perfection. This process is often difficult, but once we recognize that God is in control instead of us, mental and emotional distress becomes less overwhelming.

The world seeks to smooth the path to salvation via psychology. Christianity begins with salvation and then fosters mental health by providing an accurate description of reality. The world begins with great hope and ends in frustration; Christians begin with the frustrating reality of sin and end with great hope.

The world, however, is not quite ready to throw in the towel. Though non-Christians' efforts to improve themselves and thereby work out their own salvation are fruitless, admitting defeat would mean admitting inherent sinfulness and humbling themselves before God. Rather than accepting this, many non-Christians choose to focus on the topic of the next chapter: improving man's environment.

DODGING RESPONSIBILITY

At first glance, this seems odd. If man is capable of rescuing himself, as every non-Christian believes, then why worry about the world around you? All your efforts should be focused on self. Why abandon the virtue of selfishness?

Why? Because it does not work. Selfishness, self-esteem, efforts to avoid guilt and suffering—all these things fail the non-Christian, leaving them unredeemed and deeper in despair. And unless this despair drives the non-Christian to Christ, they must dodge responsibility for failing to rescue themselves by finding something else to blame. That something else is the same thing Frankenstein blames when he says, "Am I to be thought the only criminal, when all humankind sinned against me?"[60] If the individual is not to blame for his failure to save himself, then his environment—other people and the world around him—must be at fault. Thus, non-Christians often busy themselves wriggling out of responsibility and calling for changes in society.

The need to dodge responsibility is almost a mania in modern America. Stella Liebeck buys coffee at a McDonald's drive-through, spills some in her lap and burns herself, and a jury awards her $3 million.[61] It wasn't her fault—it was the fault of big business! An FBI agent is fired for stealing money from his agency and losing it on bets, and a judge rules that he must be re-hired by the agency because he is a victim of compulsive gambling.[62] It wasn't his fault—he has a disease! After a 1977 blackout in New York City triggered widespread looting, President Jimmy Carter concluded that, "Obviously the number one contributing factor to crime . . . is high unemployment among young people . . ."[63] It wasn't our fault—nobody would give us a job! Our litigation-mad society wants a scapegoat for every bad decision a person makes— which makes sense, if man is basically good. Our bad actions and bad decisions, if we are fundamentally innocent, must be imposed upon us by the world around us; people who do bad things must be victims of bad circumstances. My failure to save myself doesn't result from sin, so it must result from an environment that keeps me from getting in touch with my basic goodness.

This hatred of responsibility only extends so far, of course. Non-Christians are more than willing to take responsibility for their actions—when they behave well. If Stella Liebeck accidentally spilled coffee in McDonald's and it caused an escaping thief to slip, and the business owner wanted to reward her for her part in apprehending the criminal, you can bet that Stella would take responsibility for her action. "For you notice," says Lewis, "that it's only for our bad behaviour that we find all these explanations. We put our *bad* temper down to being tired or worried or hungry; we put our good temper down to ourselves."[64]

Grabbing credit and dodging blame, however, makes man less than he really is. As the next chapter explains, the man who cannot take responsibility for his bad behavior becomes only a puppet manipulated by the government or finances or the way he was disciplined as a child or the food he ate for breakfast. Dodging responsibility requires diminishing free will—until man becomes a helpless victim determined by his environment. Christianity, on the other hand, "takes sin seriously" according to Kilpatrick because "it takes people seriously."[65] The Christian worldview treats man as a creature accountable to his Creator who must be reconciled to that Creator so that he can learn to willfully follow God. This ennobles man, causing him to take both credit and blame— but only when they are due.

Christianity is not a close cousin to any other worldview. The Christian understanding of the nature of man is radically different, which in turn affects our understanding of every other aspect of reality.[66] To the extent that Christians have tried to integrate secular psychological concepts into our worldview, we have corrupted our understanding of reality. It is time for the Christian to recognize, with Kilpatrick, that "The self fails, and it fails patently, time after time. Others fail us as well. The plain truth is, when these fail, psychology has nothing left to offer."[67] As Christians recognize this, we will be able to be more effective in helping others cope with guilt and suffering. As non-Christians recognize this, they must either admit their sinfulness and embrace Christ, or continue to proclaim their goodness and blame their failures on their environment.

Moderns are "dreaming of systems so perfect that no one will need to be good."[1]
—T.S. Eliot

CHAPTER 5

A More Perfect Union

A s an American atheist at the dawn of the twentieth century, Margaret Sanger believed that man must save himself and that Darwin showed the way. In order for society to become perfect, she thought, the human race would have to rid itself of all its unfit members.

Sanger was not alone in her beliefs, of course—other atheists like Francis Galton, Adolf Hitler, George Bernard Shaw, and Herbert Spencer felt the same way. But she had a particularly vehement way of expressing herself, and the fruit of her labor is perhaps even more horrifying than Hitler's.

Sanger began by saying that the unfit—people she called "human weeds"—should not be allowed to reproduce. The poor, the uneducated, the mentally handicapped, and anyone who happened to belong to the wrong race, were hopelessly diluting the stock of humanity, and had to be stopped. People who didn't believe this were "benign imbeciles, who encourage the defective and diseased elements of humanity in their reckless and irresponsible swarming and spawning."[2]

This "spawning" had to cease, so that the fit members of society could create a generation of more highly evolved humans, who would in turn create another even more highly evolved generation. By allowing only the fit to reproduce, you could ensure that the world would progress toward perfection.

Accordingly, people who helped the less fortunate were actually undermining humanity's efforts to improve itself. Sanger spoke of the "cruelty of charity" and said that instead of charity we should "eliminate the stocks" that were most detrimental "to the future of the race and the world."[3] "If we must have welfare," she said, "give it to the rich, not to the poor."[4]

Though most people take birth control for granted today, Sanger was one of the people most responsible for encouraging its widespread use—specifically because she believed it should be used to curtail the reproduction of the unfit. She was unwilling to rely completely on this solution for the "problem," however, and so she also supported the Third Reich's policies regarding euthanasia, abortion, infanticide, and sterilization (including forced sterilization).[5] In one of the most tragic chapters in American history, leaders in the early twentieth century created "voluntary" sterilization programs that were intended primarily for the use of the poor and the weak. As Christian author Ian Taylor explains, these programs weren't always as voluntary as they pretended to be:

> Between 1907 and 1938, sterilization laws
> were passed in thirty American states, and the
> surgical operation (tubal ligation for women
> and vasectomy, or even castration, for men)
> carried out on a volunteer basis at first, but
> "voluntary" tended to become "forced," especially for those regarded as degenerate,
> defective, or criminal.[6]

While Sanger did not hesitate to impose her will on others, she made it clear that no one should impose their will on her.

She published a newspaper called *The Woman Rebel* which featured the slogan "No Gods! No Masters!" Before she married for the second time, she required her husband to sign a pre-nuptial agreement that guaranteed her right to entertain guests of either sex in her chambers at any time, day or night. Her lifestyle and her writing made it clear that she, as one of the fittest, could dictate policy to the rest of the world.

Though many people haven't heard of Sanger, it's not for lack of effort on the part of modern liberals. She is revered by many and her memory has been honored in various ways, including a recent induction into the Arizona Hall of Fame. While the Christian might expect atheists and other non-Christians to be embarrassed by Sanger's racism and her support of Hitler, many embrace her as an important pioneer in the process of improving society.

Margaret Sanger is beloved in certain circles primarily because she was the founder of Planned Parenthood, the largest abortion provider in the world today.[7] In keeping with her worldview, Sanger believed that abortion was a necessary and practical method for regulating the stock of the next generation. The evil initiated by Sanger has swollen into the abomination known as the pro-choice movement.

Sanger's vision and her legacy are completely consistent with her belief in the monster of Frankenstein. If man must save himself, individuals need to improve themselves *and* individuals need to improve the world in which they live. By lobbying for the elimination of the unfit, Sanger believed that she was helping man to achieve utopia—which, for the atheist, is the only possible salvation.

Not every member of the Frankenstein crowd would agree with Sanger's methods or rhetoric, of course, but every non-

Christian must admit that she was right about the need to improve society. Since basically good individuals—even those individuals guided by psychology—fail to perfect themselves, the fault must lie in their environment. Every non-Christian believes that if certain things were changed about society, man would have an easier time working out his own salvation.

IMPROVING PEOPLE BY IMPROVING THEIR ENVIRONMENT

Atheists are usually the most adamant about the need to improve society. Carl Rogers says that "experience leads me to believe that it is cultural influences which are the major factor in our evil behaviors."[8] Abraham Maslow agrees: "Sick people are made by a sick culture; healthy people are made possible by a healthy culture."[9] These statements summarize the typical atheistic perspective, even though Maslow and Rogers often shied away from some of the implications of atheism. Though they rejected the strict behaviorism of B.F. Skinner, both psychologists understood enough of their worldviews to assert that man is nothing more than a highly-evolved animal whose actions result largely from his response to the world around him. If this is the case, the world must change before man can change significantly.

Consistent atheists like Skinner go farther. They don't believe that the environment is a primary factor affecting the way men behave; they believe it is the *only* factor. If behaviorism is true, as atheism implies it should be, then an individual's behavior is *always* determined by stimuli imposed upon him by his environment. Thus, Skinner makes his autobiographical character Frazier proclaim, "[M]en are made good or bad and wise or foolish by the environment in which they grow."[10] Skinner trusts that the people who properly understand behaviorism can tinker with environmental stimuli to make men behave differently: "We must expect to discover that what a man does is the result of specifiable conditions and that once these conditions have been discovered, we can anticipate and to some extent determine his actions."[11]

Skinner and other behaviorists believe that they can perfect the environment and make man perfect. Ivan Pavlov, the behaviorist famous for his experiments with dogs, predicts,

> The chief, strongest, and ever-present impression received from the study of the higher nervous activity by our method is the extreme plasticity of this activity, its immense possibilities: nothing remains stationary, unyielding; and everything could always be attained, all could be changed for the better, were only the appropriate conditions realised.[12]

Skinner is even more blunt: "[T]here is no reason why progress toward a world in which people may be automatically good should be impeded."[13] According to a consistent atheistic worldview, scientists like Skinner can design a world where men and women have no choice but to behave properly. For the behaviorist, the most important thing anyone can do is help change society.[14]

Non-Christians who aren't atheists put less emphasis on changing society, but they still blame man's environment for much of the crime and unkindness that plague our world. Non-Christian worldviews like Islam or Mormonism often make it sound as though man is solely responsible for his actions—but they still must ultimately assert that man's tendency to behave badly originates outside of man, in his environment. Even the New Age proponent, who believes that everyone is god and seems to place the onus for achieving salvation squarely on the individual's shoulders, admits that a better society would help people get in touch with their godhood. New Age proponents long for a society that won't place limits on people, so that people won't have to acknowledge any authority other than themselves. "If you promise to feel or behave by a certain set of rules," says Shakti Gawain, "eventually you are going to have to choose between being true to yourself and being true to those rules."[15] To avoid this dilemma, the New Age adherent hopes for a society that doesn't require any obedience to rules—namely, anarchy.

But is anarchy really best? Marxists call for just the opposite: a dictatorship. Other worldviews demand other changes. How can anyone know exactly what is meant by a "better society"?

That's the rub. While every non-Christian believes that society needs to be improved, many have radically different ideas about what constitutes an improvement. A Mormon might believe outlawing caffeine, tobacco and alcohol would remove temptation and improve our environment; a New Age proponent might believe legalizing marijuana would make things better. Non-Christians recommend improvements in all arenas, from education to the arts to city planning to nutrition to economics. Sometimes these recommendations contradict each other. Who gets to decide which recommendations to implement?

Who gets to decide? The king. In order to shape public policy, non-Christians must become involved politically. The best hope for the Mormon to outlaw caffeine, or the Muslim to outlaw Christianity, or the New Age proponent to outlaw laws, is to create the laws themselves. The best hope for the non-Christian to improve the world the *right* way (his way) is to sit on the throne.

MAKING THE RULES

V.I. Lenin, the first leader of the Soviet Union, understood this. Although Marxism claims that a society's economic system determines its political system, culture, and even the thoughts of its people, Lenin did not believe he could start Russia on the path to communism by changing his country's economics. Instead, he seized political power and then used that power to dictate "improvements" in economics, religion, etc. Lenin believed that every country must first establish a "dictatorship of the proletariat" that would give the common man the authority to seize all private property. Until the dictatorship was established, Marxists would have little hope of mustering the power to change the economic system and thereby move men closer to paradise.

Though other non-Christians may not talk about dictatorships, all must ultimately rely on governmental power to effect the societal changes they deem necessary. It makes sense: you can't walk into a school and demand that the Ten Commandments be removed from the wall—unless you're in charge. But if you make the rules, then you can determine the way in which we improve society. And that means you can help man save himself.

Today in America many people acknowledge that our government is immense—even some non-Christians seem suddenly disturbed by our bloated bureaucracy. But this swelling should not catch us by surprise. If man must improve society in order to achieve salvation, and if improving society requires imposing your "improvements" on people who don't agree with you, then man must use government—and use it a lot—to get his way. The history of American government in the twentieth century underscores this fact.

Some people believe that poverty causes man to lose touch with his basic goodness—then why not improve society by creating Social Security? Others believe that guns tempt men to commit crimes—why not the Brady Bill? Some people believe that we need a more vibrant cultural life—why not create a National Endowment for the Arts? Other people believe, as Horace Mann believed, in the public schools:

> Let the Common School be expanded to its
> capabilities, let it be worked with the efficiency
> of which it is susceptible, and nine-tenths of
> the crimes in the penal code would become
> obsolete; the long catalogue of human ills
> would be abridged; men would walk more
> safely by day; every pillow would be more
> inviolable by night; property, life and character
> held by a stronger tenure; all rational hopes
> respecting the future brightened.[16]

If Mann is right, it seems only logical that the government should develop state schools, and that activists should use the

National Education Association to encourage the government to make the right public policy decisions.

This list could go on and on. Though most non-Christians would deny that the government is mankind's savior, many demonstrate a faith in government that borders on fanaticism. One small step from the government, like abolishing racism via Affirmative Action or sexism via the Equal Rights Amendment, is advertised as a giant leap toward salvation for mankind. The California Task Force to Promote Self-Esteem is an excellent example of this mentality: certain people thought that they knew what was best for other citizens (learning self-esteem), but they needed the authority to *cause* these citizens to learn self-esteem. By convincing the California legislature to create a Task Force, they gained governmental authority to carry out their plan to improve society. Neil Smelser, a Task Force enthusiast, puts it this way:

> [I]t becomes essential for the leaders of society, first, to establish social conditions that will maximize the development of self-esteem among the population and, second, to establish social arrangements that will rescue and rehabilitate those who have emerged from families and communities with a sense of diminished self-worth. That is the agenda of the California Task Force . . . [17]

The "leaders" in America must "establish social conditions." In other words, those in power must enact policies that will improve society. The government becomes an important vehicle steamrolling obstacles on man's path to redemption.

T H E I N D I V I D U A L V S . S O C I E T Y

Those who become obsessed with using government to aid man's salvation, whether their original motives are to protect endangered species or put warning labels on rock albums, often end up treating society as more important than the individual. This is an especially enticing temptation for the behaviorist, because he believes that the *only* thing keeping people from being good all the time is their environment (Skinner says, "I am not trying to change people. All I want to do is change the world in which they live."[18]). This may seem like a harmless attitude—until one realizes that changing the world often means trampling a few individuals. When Skinner's autobiographical counterpart is asked about the man who doesn't want to join the perfect society—the man who just wants to be left alone—he replies, "The man has tied himself up with a moribund competitive society. All we can do is make his personal demise as painless as possible, unless he's intelligent enough to adjust to the new order."[19]

Two of the worst butchers in the twentieth century, Adolf Hitler and Joseph Stalin, both claimed to be working to save mankind, when in reality they were trampling individuals. Stalin believed that every trace of capitalism had to be erased before man's salvation—communism—could be achieved in the Soviet Union, and so he unflinchingly erased *tens of millions* of people. Hitler believed, like Sanger, that only the fittest should be allowed to survive so that mankind could achieve perfection, and so he unflinchingly erased *tens of millions* of people. What is less well-known about Hitler is that he initiated the policy for which Sanger pined: forced sterilization. "After the collapse of Hitler's thousand year Reich in 1945," writes Taylor, "the well-kept German records showed that between 1927 and 1933, about eighty-five people a year were voluntarily sterilized. Under the Nazis, at least two million human beings had been forcibly sterilized at a rate of about 450 per day."[20]

Would Hitler or Sanger still be enthusiastic about their policies if they were forced to endure the trauma and humiliation of forced sterilization? To ask such a question is to forget the virtue of selfishness—Hitler wasn't actually concerned with whether or not his programs helped other men, only that they benefited him. People who "selflessly" champion policies that hurt innocent people are not concerned about anyone except themselves and their own particular plan of salvation.

Other non-Christians (and Christians!) can also fall into this mindset, if they allow themselves to believe that the social improvement they advocate is so important that it justifies nullifying the rights of individuals. Nowhere is this more obvious than in the public schools today. Although modern liberals in America are constantly clamoring for their "right to choose," they often deny this right to parents who want to educate their children outside of the public school system. The reason? Liberals have decided, as Mann decided more than a century ago, that the best thing for children is to be educated in state schools—*even if* this means being unfair to some families. Even if some families have to pay twice for education (once with their taxes to support public schools, and once to pay private school tuition); even if those who can't afford to pay twice are forced to settle for a shoddy education; even if everyone's money is wasted on an engorged education bureaucracy;[21] state school advocates believe that the overall societal benefit outweighs the personal cost.

The bald fact is that public education fails in almost every
way that it purports to help. Forty percent of the fourth
graders in public schools failed to meet basic reading standards
in 1996.[22] Public school enthusiasts blame such results on
under-funding, forgetting the fact that New York City spends
more than $7,500 per public school student while private
schools in the same area spend about $2,500 per pupil and get
better results (the graduation rate in some area public schools
in New York is as low as 45%, while Catholic schools in the
same neighborhoods graduate 95%).[23]

These statistics do not go unnoticed by modern liberals—
President Bill Clinton wisely chose to protect his own daughter
from the public school system—but they are dismissed by
starry-eyed enthusiasts as irrelevant. Statistics, after all, just tell
you how many individuals may be suffering; public school
proponents are certain that in the long run the rewards will
justify the suffering (as long as their kids don't suffer).

I should pause here to make something clear: none of this
is meant to deride the work of committed Christians in the
public schools. We are called to be salt and light in the darkest
places, and many Christians faithfully obey this command
every day in our state schools. The problem with state schools
is not, generally speaking, the people who teach there—it is the
system itself. The assumption that the government can educate children better than parents is unbiblical, and destined to
fail. Christians should shine as bright as God lets them in the
public schools; but they should never be deceived into *believing*
in the public school system.

More on that later. For now, it's enough to understand
that non-Christians face a real temptation to be passionate
lovers of humanity, and haters of actual men. If you believe

that your social program will help everyone on their path to salvation, it's easy to impose that program without worrying about the cost to certain individuals. When such fanaticism is coupled with the ethical relativism predominant in the Frankenstein crowd, expect a recipe for disaster.

LEGAL POSITIVISM

If the Christian worldview is true, then only two worldviews (Christianity and traditional Judaism) know where to find absolute truth; every other worldview places authority in the hands of men. But placing authority in the hands of sinful men guarantees not only that ethical standards will change, but also that *laws* will change. Societies led by men who have forgotten God adopt *legal positivism*, which means that the government gets to make up the rules. Whereas Christians think that God made the rules and our leaders should enforce them, most non-Christians think that whoever is in power gets to decide what is lawful.

As *Brave New World* and *1984* and just about every good futuristic novel warn, a society where the government makes the laws is a society ripe for abusive dictators. If no standard exists outside of man, then the men in power usually become the standard. If these men are sinful, they will tip the scales of justice in their favor, harming the most vulnerable in the process. "Since there is no confidence in justice," writes Dietrich Bonhoeffer, "whatever is useful is declared to be just."[24] No policy is "useful" for everybody—for example, excessive taxation is "useful" for bureaucrats but not for the taxpayer—so the "justice" that is created in a secular society will generally prove useful for the people in power, and oppressive for the masses. The legalization of abortion demonstrates this principle: since abortion is useful for many people who govern America, it becomes a "just" option even though it deprives those without a voice in government—the unborn—of their most fundamental right.

The spate of abortion clinic bombings is a natural backlash to this legal positivism. Citizens frustrated by the injustice of legalized abortion learn to despise all governmental authority and conclude that they must take the law into their own hands (ironically, this is just another form of legal positivism—relying on the individual to dispense justice rather than God). The state responds to this backlash by exerting more authority—even if it means overstepping constitutional boundaries by stifling free speech via "bubble laws." And then the vicious cycle begins again. As Russell Kirk explains, "If the political power decrees positive laws without reference to general consent, those laws will be evaded or defied, and respect for law will diminish, so that force must be substituted for justice . . ."[25] First the government creates laws that are unjust, causing some citizens who are hurt by the injustice to ignore those laws; then the government must use force to ensure obedience which in turn precipitates more defiance from citizens . . . Injustice perpetuates injustice.

Where does it end? Alexander Solzhenitsyn, a Christian who suffered for several years in a Soviet prison camp, was imprisoned for allegedly saying something bad about Stalin, although no one proved that he said anything derogatory. He explains the mentality of those in authority in the Soviet Union:

Thence arose the most practical conclusion:
that it was useless to seek absolute evidence—
for evidence is always relative—or
unchallengeable witnesses—for they can say
different things at different times. The proofs
of guilt were *relative*, approximate, and the
interrogator could find them, even when there
was no evidence and no witness, without
leaving his office, 'basing his conclusions not
only on his own intellect but also on his Party
sensitivity, his *moral forces*' (in other words, the
superiority of someone who has slept well, has
been well fed, and has not been beaten up)
'and on his *character*' (i.e., his willingness to
apply cruelty!).[26]

Legal positivism may begin with fine-sounding phrases like
"the will of the people" or "the good of the community," but it
ends with rulers accumulating enough power to openly disdain
justice. If everything is relative, then justice is relative to the
whims of the rulers.

Ultimately, the Frankenstein crowd ends where they began:
with pride. Because non-Christians begin with the prideful
assertion that man is good enough to save himself, they end
with the prideful assertion that, if elected, they can create
justice. Though it may seem arrogant to believe that you know
how to govern better than anyone else, many non-Christians
believe exactly that. Why shouldn't they? They believe (as
Christians believe) that they adhere to the one true worldview,
and their worldview (unless they are Jewish) requires them to
adopt legal positivism. If man must make the laws, who better

to make the laws than the people who *really* understand how to rescue man? It's only natural for Buddhists to think Buddhists should be in charge and Jehovah's Witnesses to think Jehovah's Witnesses should be in charge. If your worldview is the right worldview, and someone's got to make up the rules, it might as well be someone who adheres to your worldview.

The non-Christian may respond by saying that Christians believe the same thing—but that isn't exactly true. Yes, Christians would like to see Christians running the government, but we expect our leaders only to acknowledge God's law and enforce it, rather than *create* law. The difference is as vast as the difference between justice and injustice, as we shall see in a moment.

For now, it's enough to recognize the arrogance inherent in a man who believes that he and his like-minded friends can create law for an entire nation. Although other citizens adhering to other worldviews might whole-heartedly disagree with his laws, he must assume that they are at best misinformed, and possibly stupid or criminal. In short, the man who presumes to create law must be an *elitist* who believes that he and his fellow disciples are wiser and more moral than the rest of humanity.

THE SUPREME COURT KNOWS BEST

Fyodor Dostoyevsky describes just such an elitist in his novel *The Devils*. This character, an atheist, believes that the way to establish utopia is to

> divide humanity into two unequal parts. One-tenth is to be granted absolute freedom and

unrestricted powers over the remaining nine-
tenths. Those must give up their individuality
and be turned into something like a herd, and
by their boundless obedience, will by a series of
regenerations attain a state of primeval innocence, something like the original paradise.[27]

In other words, most of mankind is too stupid to save themselves, but the elite can rescue them if only they will obey.

Skinner echoes this attitude through his autobiographical
character, Frazier. Toward the end of *Walden Two*, Frazier
assumes the position of the crucifixion and discusses his
similarities to God:

When we ask what Man can make of Man, we
don't mean the same thing by 'Man' in both
instances. We mean to ask what a few men can
make of mankind. And that's the all-absorbing
question of the twentieth century. What kind
of world can we build—those of us who
understand the science of behavior?[28]

Variations of this elitism appear far too often in real life in
recent centuries. Sanger and Hitler both provide gruesome
examples, although their versions of elitism required them not
to rescue the vulnerable, but to kill them and rescue the strong.
Another influential atheist, Voltaire, believed only superior
beings like himself could adhere to atheism and still act morally: "I want my lawyer, tailor, valets, even my wife, to believe
in God; I think that if they do I shall be robbed less and
cheated less."[29] Elites like himself could know the truth and

govern those people incapable of dealing with the truth.

Corliss Lamont, a Humanist, believes that "'the moral obligation to be intelligent' ranks always among the highest of duties."[30] The implication, of course, is that those who are not intelligent—according to Lamont's definition—are not fit to lead. Sigmund Freud viewed most people as unfit: "In the depths of my heart I can't help being convinced that my dear fellow men, with a few exceptions, are worthless."[31]

Although atheists are most susceptible to elitism, it can infect any non-Christian. Even Benjamin Franklin was not immune:

> There seems to me at present to be great
> occasion for raising a united party for virtue,
> by forming the virtuous and good men of all
> nations into a regular body, to be governed by
> suitable good and wise rules, which good and
> wise men may probably be more unanimous in
> their obedience to than common people are to
> common laws.[32]

Naturally, Franklin considered himself to be one of those "good and wise" people who could create better rules than most people.

Elitism is alive and well in America today. Ginger Pace, a grandmother and public school teacher, discovered this when she put up a bulletin board in her classroom to celebrate Thanksgiving. At the top she placed the words, "Thank you, God, for . . ." Two of her co-workers complained, so an assistant principal told her to take down her bulletin board. When she refused, they told her she had broken the law because she was imposing her religion on others.

What law? As Pace points out, "Thanksgiving is a national holiday set aside by Congress to give thanks to God. . . . From the first president of the United States to the current one, Thanksgiving Proclamations have been given to the people. President Clinton's 1996 proclamation said, 'We still—and always—raise our voices in prayer to God, thanking him in humility for the countless blessings he has bestowed on our nation and our people.'"[33] At the creation of the United States Constitution, delegates at an impasse joined in prayer to seek God's guidance. The modern version of separation of church and state is not an unchanging principle handed down to us by God or even by our forefathers; rather, it is a new rule *created* by an elite group to help the masses avoid being confused by religion. Forget "Father Knows Best"—the Supreme Court knows best, and has decided that an education that includes God only hinders man's efforts to rescue himself.

Secular elites have amassed political power in America to the extent that they, rather than parents, control the education of the next generation. Many of these elites would like to remove the burden of child-rearing from parents altogether, as Skinner recommends in *Walden Two*: "Group care is better than parental care. . . . The control of behavior is an intricate science, into which the average mother could not be initiated without years of training. . . . Home is not the place to raise children."[34] Sound Orwellian? Attorney General Janet Reno sounds the same way when she insists that the government should play an active role in child development "in the critical years between birth and age three."[35] University of Wisconsin-Madison professor Jack Westman actually recommends that the state license parents! In his book *Licensing Parents: Can We Prevent Child Abuse and Neglect?* he makes the case that licenses will rip out the "root causes" of crime, which he believes are found in "incompetent parenting."[36]

Is it any wonder that government swells bigger and bigger? If society needs to be improved to rescue man, and different people with different views must all use governmental authority to create the rules to improve society, then the state inevitably balloons into King Kong. Remember when you were a kid choosing sides to play football? If the other team began to look too powerful and certain of winning, more and more kids would scramble to join that team—until the winning side featured forty of the best athletes and the losing side was just a few stubborn scrubs. The Frankenstein crowd knows who has the power—the government—and they want to make sure they're helping guide that side to victory—that is, salvation.

PROMOTING JUSTICE

In contrast, the Hyde crowd does not believe that they can use government to raise better children or wipe out poverty or initiate utopia. The Hyde crowd doesn't believe that they can invent even one good law. Instead, Christians think that government should be based on God's law, and that government should do just one thing: promote justice. Romans 13:1-5 spells out the proper role of the state:

> Everyone must submit himself to the governing authorities, for there is no authority except that which God has established. The authori-

ties that exist have been established by God.
Consequently, he who rebels against the
authority is rebelling against what God has
instituted, and those who do so will bring
judgment on themselves. For rulers hold no
terror for those who do right, but for those
who do wrong. Do you want to be free from
fear of the one in authority? Then do what is
right and he will commend you. For he is
God's servant to do you good. But if you do
wrong, be afraid, for he does not bear the
sword for nothing. He is God's servant, an
agent of wrath to bring punishment on the
wrong-doer. Therefore, it is necessary to
submit to the authorities, not only because of
possible punishment but also because of
conscience.

What is government good for? According to scripture, good
government focuses strictly on protecting the innocent and
punishing the guilty. Government is neither nanny nor parent
nor savior—it is God's agent for promoting justice on earth.

Justice can only exist in a society based on an unchanging
standard for law. Men change and the laws they create change;
the God of the Bible is the only unchanging foundation (1
Samuel 15:29) upon which law can remain fixed. Injustice
doesn't matter much to those who wield power in society—
they can always ensure that they receive their due, and more.
The people to whom justice matters most are the poor and the
powerless, who will only be treated fairly if an unchanging
standard requires it. "Above all," writes G.K. Chesterton, "if

we wish to protect the poor we shall be in favour of fixed rules and clear dogmas. The *rules* of a club are occasionally in favour of the poor member. The drift of a club is always in favour of the rich one."[37] It is the same with government: the powerless can only win a court battle with the powerful if power has nothing to do with it—that is, if justice reigns.

Most non-Christians can offer no reason for *not* showing favor to the rich or powerful or brilliant, because their worldviews encourage elitism. Sanger was completely consistent with the Frankenstein view: the elite must be closer to salvation than the rest of mankind, and therefore they should make the rules. Chesterton reminds us that "Only the Christian Church can offer any rational objection to a complete confidence in the rich. For she has maintained from the beginning that the danger was not in man's environment, but in man."[38] If you're a non-Christian, it makes sense to follow the rich and famous, because they live in the best environment and therefore should be the most in touch with their goodness. "If better conditions will make the poor more fit to govern themselves," Chesterton continues, "why should not better conditions already make the rich more fit to govern them? On the ordinary environment argument the matter is fairly manifest. The comfortable class must be merely our vanguard in Utopia."[39] Only Christians dispute this, claiming that the strongest king and the smartest scientist are just as dead in their sins as every other unredeemed man.

The Christian wants to level the playing field. Justice shouldn't be for sale, and those in power shouldn't get extra helpings. Everyone should receive according to his due, as God commands in Exodus 23:2-3, 6-9:

> Do not follow the crowd in doing wrong.
> When you give testimony in a lawsuit, do not
> pervert justice by siding with the crowd, and
> do not show favoritism to a poor man in his
> lawsuit. . . . Do not deny justice to your poor
> people in their lawsuits. Have nothing to do
> with a false charge and do not put an innocent
> or honest person to death, for I will not acquit
> the guilty. Do not accept a bribe, for a bribe
> blinds those who see and twists the words of
> the righteous. Do not oppress an alien; you
> yourselves know how it feels to be aliens,
> because you were aliens in Egypt.

Look closely: this is the kind of world each of us dreams about. Though earth will always be a distant second to heaven, it could be vastly improved if governments actually dispensed true justice. Such an improvement will not redeem a single man, but it would make a nation more pleasing to God—something that will matter very much to that nation on the Day of Judgment.

While the Frankenstein faith tends toward elitist governments, the Hyde faith encourages nations that promote justice. "If we wish to pull down the prosperous oppressor," says Chesterton, "we cannot do it with the new doctrine of human perfectibility; we can do it with the old doctrine of Original Sin."[40] The fall of the Iron Curtain made Chesterton look like a prophet, as Barbara von der Heydt explains: "I discovered that in many cases the Christians were the moral leaders of the peaceful revolution [that led to the downfall of the Soviet Union]: they set the tone for it, and they were decisive in keeping the confrontation nonviolent. Their courage and leadership galvanized a far broader movement."[41] If law is relative, the people who make the laws are always in the right; only law based on God's unchanging nature can condemn guilty leaders.

When Christians seek to apply their faith to politics, they should take the advice of former president Calvin Coolidge: "Don't hesitate to be as reactionary as the multiplication table."[42] Rulers may invent countless laws denying that three times three equals nine, but that basic fact will never change— just as moral truth never changes. Abortion is still murder, no matter how many Supreme Court justices think it is acceptable. Failure to recognize this fundamental moral truth causes more societal failings, as Bonhoeffer explains: "The distinction between life that is worth living and life that is not worth living must sooner or later destroy life itself."[43] Only Christianity can guide a nation away from this pit, and teach it to administer justice.

History confirms this. In a tale of two Revolutions, we find all the differences between Hyde and Frankenstein.

Two Revolutions

Although the American Revolution and the French Revolution occurred about the same time in history and occasionally generated support from the same people (most notably Thomas Paine), one resulted in freedom and one in tyranny. The difference? The monster in which you believe. Bonhoeffer writes,

> The American Revolution was almost contemporary with the French one, and politically the

two were not unconnected; yet they were profoundly different in character. The American democracy is not founded upon the emancipated man, but quite on the contrary, upon the kingdom of God and the limitation of all earthly powers by the sovereignty of God. It is indeed significant when, in contrast to the *Declaration of the Rights of Man*, American historians can say that the federal constitution was written by men who were conscious of original sin and of the wickedness of the human heart.[44]

Russell Kirk agrees:

A principal difference between the American Revolution and the French Revolution was this: the American revolutionaries in general held a biblical view of man and his bent toward sin, while the French Revolutionaries in general attempted to substitute for the biblical understanding an optimistic doctrine of human goodness advanced by the philosophes of the rationalistic Enlightenment. The American view led to the Constitution of 1787; the French view, to the Terror and to a new autocracy.[45]

The lie that Christianity has nothing to say to "secular" concerns like politics is blasted to bits at the very start of United States history. While French revolutionaries believed that they could create the proper society by overthrowing the privileged class, thereby allowing man to behave in accord with his basic goodness all the time, American revolutionaries generally assumed that man was inherently sinful, and that the best form of government would take this sinfulness into account.

Which view matched reality? The French optimism led to the gross injustice of the guillotine, where victims were executed simply to please a bloodthirsty mob. The American "pessimism" led to liberty and justice—not a perfect society, but one in which power is not easily abused.

American "pessimism" mandated the creation of a *democratic republic*. Many people today refer to America as a democracy; they are wrong. It would be much more accurate to describe France during her revolution as a democracy, because pure democracy is nothing more than mob rule. If America were a democracy, women could "get out the vote" and lawfully enslave men, since men are in the minority. Democracy allows the majority to consistently impose its will upon various minorities, because democracy places power in the hands of the 51%. Any policy, no matter how absurd or brutal, becomes legal if enough people vote for it.

In contrast, law in a republic is based upon a written document that codifies God's natural law. The United States Constitution was created to serve this purpose—to check rulers' tendencies to create law rather than govern according to God's law. In America, laws must be *constitutional*—that is, they must dovetail with the fixed law articulated in the Constitution. Judges should be America's watchdogs guarding against legal positivism, overturning laws that are based on man's whims rather than on God's foundation.

Of course, it doesn't always work that way. Today the

Supreme Court has not only abandoned its watchdog role, it now leads the charge toward positivism. But this reversal only underscores mankind's need for a government like the one initially created by the founding fathers. Why build a republic? Because politicians are sinful people who would rather create rules than abide by them. America's founders understood this.

This understanding also resulted in the separation of powers. America features three distinct branches of government: the legislative, the judiciary, and the executive. When this system works, Congress articulates laws, the Supreme Court judges whether or not the laws are constitutional, and the White House enforces them. Many "checks and balances" built into this system help distribute power, making it difficult for any person or group to amass too much. For example, the President may nominate Supreme Court justices, but the nominations must be approved by Congress—ensuring that the President cannot wield too much influence over the judiciary.

If man is basically good, the founding fathers wasted their time crafting this system of checks and balances; there would be little reason to worry about leaders accumulating power. But if man is sinful, as almost every founding father except Franklin and Paine believed, such a system is not only sensible, it's mandatory. James Madison, often called the Father of the Constitution, speaks for the Hyde crowd when he writes,

> But the great security against a gradual concentration of the several powers in the same department, consists in giving to those who administer each department, the necessary

constitutional means, and personal motives, to
resist encroachments of the others. . . . Ambition must be made to counteract ambition. . . .
It may be a reflection on human nature, that
such devices should be necessary to control the
abuses of government. But what is government itself, but the greatest of all reflection on
human nature? If men were angels, no government would be necessary. If angels were to
govern men, neither external nor internal
controls on government would be necessary.
In framing a government, which is to be
administered by men over men, the great
difficulty lies in this: You must first enable the
government to control the governed; and in
the next place, oblige it to control itself.[46]

It's interesting to note that Christianity pervaded colonial
America to the extent that many non-Christians, including
Thomas Jefferson, often acknowledged the sinfulness of man.
Kirk tells us that "Jefferson, rationalist though he was, declared
that in matters of political power, one must not trust in the
alleged goodness of man, but 'bind him down with the chains
of the Constitution.'"[47]

Madison and Jefferson knew enough about themselves to
mistrust themselves. We "have not got to crown the exceptional man who knows he can rule," says Chesterton. "Rather
we must crown the much more exceptional man who knows he
can't."[48] For the most part, America's founding fathers fell into
this second category. They understood that they were sinful
and that they would, given the chance, abuse political power.

Their unwillingness to entrust even exceptional men—and even themselves—with substantial power was the key difference between the French and American revolutions.

Both the French and the American revolutionaries wanted liberty, but they did not want the same thing. Most Americans simply wanted liberty from an intrusive government, so that their rights would not be infringed upon unless they broke the law. The French wanted absolute liberty, because they believed that man would never act immorally in the proper environment. America's simpler aspirations led to simple liberties, while the French's lofty hopes led to tyranny: in the French Revolution, says Bonhoeffer, we find

> an underlying law of history, namely that the
> demand for absolute liberty brings men to the
> depths of slavery. The master of the machine
> becomes its slave. . . . The emancipation of the
> masses leads to the reign of terror and the
> guillotine. . . . The liberation of man as an
> absolute ideal leads only to man's self-destruc-
> tion.[49]

If man is perfectible, the French experiment should have borne delicious fruit—but it yielded death. Only the American experiment led to a measure of life, liberty, and the pursuit of happiness.

None of this, of course, is meant to imply that America is a perfect society enabling men to achieve salvation. As with every form of government, the United States' political system has problems—and it always will. No political system can magically erase man's sinfulness; on earth we must settle for government that is good at keeping sinfulness in check. The American form of government, as it was originally conceived, proved effective at providing liberty while maintaining order. This effectiveness is gradually diminishing; but the failure is not the fault of the system—it's the fault of the people within the system.

LIBERTY VS. LICENSE

More and more, Americans have learned to abuse their liberty. Today most Americans will demand their rights at the drop of a coffee cup, but very few are willing to admit their responsibilities. This attitude is disastrous if man is sinful, because liberty may only be preserved in a fallen world by faithfully carrying out corresponding duties. People cannot exercise absolute liberty; instead, they must limit their liberties by using their rights *responsibly*. The classic example is our right to free speech—we have the right to say what we will, but only if we are responsible enough not to yell "Fire!" in a crowded theater. Each right is limited by various responsibilities. Failure to behave responsibly will result in the loss of liberty, as Edmund Burke understood:

> Men are qualified for civil liberty, in exact proportion to their disposition to put moral chains upon their own appetites . . . Society cannot exist unless a controlling power upon will and appetite be placed somewhere, and the less of it there is within, the more there must be without. It is ordained in the eternal constitution of things, that men of intemperate

minds cannot be free. Their passions forge
their fetters.[50]

Ironically, the best way for Americans to maximize their liberty
is to put limits on it themselves. If citizens don't control
themselves, the government will be forced to control them.

It sounds at this point like Christianity is on a crash course
with tyranny. If man cannot control himself—and that's the
Christian view of man—then government must control him.
Doesn't it follow logically that Christians should embrace
totalitarianism to control man's selfish appetites?

To ask this is to forget the good news. Christ's work on
the cross sets men free from their sinfulness, and by the power
of the Holy Spirit they can behave responsibly. National
liberty requires a moral citizenry, and only God can make man
moral. Alexis de Tocqueville asked the right questions more
than a century ago: "How is it possible that society should
escape destruction if the moral tie is not strengthened in
proportion as the political tie is relaxed? And what can be
done with a people who are their own masters if they are not
submissive to the Deity?"[51] What can be done? The question
haunts us today: Americans still have corporate liberty, but
many are enslaved by sin. And sinful behavior undermines
liberty.

Does this mean that liberty will be in jeopardy where *any*
citizens sin? Of course. We live in an imperfect world, where
corporate liberty is tenuous. But that doesn't mean that every
man, woman, and child in America must become a Christian
to preserve our freedom. Such a hope is unrealistic, and it also
assumes that Christians never sin, which is absurd. More
importantly, it overlooks the fact that God can bring about

good even when men or demons get in the way.

Men can never be perfect enough to ensure liberty, but we may, by the grace of God, take steps to avoid tyranny. Put simply, we have no guarantees of corporate liberty in this world, but we do have the guarantee that societies that forget God are destined for tyranny (Proverbs 28:12, 15-16). To avoid tyranny, then, those Americans who are Christians must behave like salt and light, so that the American culture begins to manifest the "taste" and "look" of Christianity. If the slaves—those enslaved to sin—lead the culture, whether in government, the arts, philosophy, or education, we can be certain our corporate liberty will vanish. If Christians lead the culture, we can be certain at least that we are not certain of tyranny.

This holds true not only in America, but around the world. "Both the East and the West," writes von der Heydt, "are confronted with the same need. No society can live harmoniously in responsible freedom without acknowledging and renewing its moral roots."[52] There will always be people within a society unwilling to acknowledge morality, of course, but these people should not be leading. The leaders of a culture should recognize moral truth, and—ideally—enjoy the God-given freedom to live in accord with that truth.

Christians will always be more concerned with changing hearts than changing laws, and this is as it should be. Changed laws can only coerce men to behave decently; changed hearts can cause men to behave well without giving up their political liberty. "The people cannot look to legislation generally for success," warns Coolidge. "Industry, thrift, character, are not conferred by act or resolve."[53] People learn to live responsibly by the power of the Holy Spirit, not by the power of Congress.

The Christian cares about politics because God expects him to, but the Christian should never mistake the government for his savior. No government will ever eradicate poverty or make everyone behave morally, because we live in a fallen world. When government seeks to redeem society it only makes things worse; only Christ can improve things dramatically. The Christian should simply see to it that government does its job—promoting justice—and then look for other answers to other problems.

The tragedy of abortion illustrates this principle. Christians certainly should work fervently to outlaw abortion, because part of the government's job is to protect the innocent. But outlawing abortion will not stop every mother from killing her child, because people can still choose to break the law. The best way to guard against abortion is to lead people to Christ, so that they understand God's moral order and have the power to obey. Changing the law might just make people travel farther to kill their baby; changing hearts can cause people to protect their children even with an abortion clinic around the corner.

In short, Christians should not expect government to be what it cannot be. God ordained government to promote justice; Christians should help government fulfill this role. But Christians should never confuse the government's role with the role of the family, the church, or God.

LEADING BY SERVING

Christians believe that God gave *jurisdiction* over various arenas to various earthly institutions, and that each of these institutions ultimately fall under God's jurisdiction, as

Bonhoeffer acknowledges: "It is God's will that there shall be . . . marriage, government and church in the world; and it is His will that all these, each in its own way, shall be through Christ, directed towards Christ, and in Christ."[54] God created the state to promote justice, the family to nurture and educate, and the church to exalt, edify, and evangelize. When any institution oversteps its own rightful jurisdiction, the balance of power teeters.

Today, examples of the American government overstepping her jurisdiction abound. Are people hungry? Although God expects families and the church to care for them, welfare steps in. Do kids need an education? Although God expects parents to oversee the education of their children (Proverbs 22:6), the public schools step in (recently NEA assistant general counsel Michael Simpson claimed that "there is no such thing as a fundamental parental right."[55]). Families and churches see their ability to impact society minimized by an intrusive state.

The more the state intrudes, the closer we move to tyranny. William Kilpatrick warns, "One thing you notice about totalitarian states is that they have little use for the family or the parish or the local government."[56] In a sinful world, centralized power is dangerous because it is easy to abuse. As the government grabs more and more authority, it sets the stage for totalitarianism.

It would be nice if Christians could blame the present situation entirely on the government's lust for power—but this simply isn't true. To some extent the government is simply picking up slack, taking over arenas that families and the church have abdicated. If the church was doing a good job ministering to the needy, and families took more responsibility for their children's education, the state would have little excuse for intruding. Unfortunately, the church and the family often yawn and get out of the way.

How can Christians reverse this trend? Many have already started. Some are involved in politics, working to keep the government focused on its own role. Many others are "standing in the gap"—helping the church and families re-assume responsibility for arenas in their jurisdiction. Most importantly, Christians are learning to "lead by serving." Instead of clamoring for their rights and seeking a bigger slice of governmental power, Christians are fulfilling the obligations that have been ignored for too long by churches and families. As these institutions again take responsibility for their jurisdiction, non-Christians may notice that following Christ results in a radically different attitude toward power—that Christ tells His followers, "The greatest among you should be like the youngest, and the one who rules like the one who serves" (Luke 22:26).

As Christians lead by serving, they can expect opposition. Now that politicians have accumulated much of the authority that rightfully belongs to the other institutions, they will be reluctant to let go. Hundreds of thousands of people's jobs depend upon the government staying involved in education and welfare; many of these people will perceive attacks on governmental intrusion as attacks on their livelihood. Predictions are usually risky—but there are certain things it is safe to expect as we look toward the twenty-first century: The homeschool movement will come under increasing fire for their efforts to restore jurisdiction over education to the family; various Christian charities will also draw fire for "undermining" the welfare system; and Christians in general will be told, as William Wilberforce was told 200 hundred years ago when he sought to outlaw the slave trade in England, "Things have come to a pretty pass when religion is allowed to invade public life."[57]

In spite of such opposition, Christians must hold fast to Christ, following Him in both their private and public lives. While the world clings to their faith in Frankenstein and seeks to improve society to help save mankind, Christians seek to improve society simply to please God. And even if Christians improve society beyond their wildest dreams, they must remember that their efforts have not moved a single man or woman closer to redemption. People aren't redeemed by society, and they certainly aren't redeemed in groups. A man passes from death to life as an *individual* in relationship with Jesus Christ.

PEOPLE MATTER

Although non-Christians often consider societal schemes more important than the individual, Christians must scrupulously avoid this lie. No man can save the world, even with the best and biggest plan for government. There is no hope for mankind in general, only for mankind in specific—as individuals surrender their lives to Jesus Christ. Christians must condemn the lie that society is more important than the individual first, because this lie ruins societies, as Bonhoeffer explains:

> For [certain non-Christians] the individual is only a means to an end in the service of the community. The happiness of the community takes precedence over the natural right of the

individual. This means in principle the proclamation of social eudemonism and the
curtailment of all the rights of individuals. But
this constitutes an attack on natural life itself,
and the destruction of the rights of the individual paves the way for the destruction of all
rights without exception; this is the way to
chaos.[58]

More importantly, Christians must condemn this lie because it
can cause us to forget that Christ died not to redeem court-
houses or races or school districts, but individual people like
the woman shouting at you at the city council meeting. Lewis
says it best: "[T]o the Christian, individuals are more important, for they live eternally; and races, civilizations and the like,
are in comparison the creatures of a day."[59] Individuals are
eternal beings who will spend eternity *somewhere*; the "where"
should matter to them and certainly matters to God. The
White House will crumble, the Grand Canyon will crumble,
America will crumble—but the little boy who threw a baseball
through your window will go on living forever and ever. No
political plan or educational objective will determine where;
only His personal relationship with Christ determines that.
And so *he* matters far more than any plan or objective.

Dorothy Sayers tells a story that includes "an untidy
woman" who thinks that all man needs is a better environment, and then he can be redeemed: "So perplexing. And just
to think that we have been quite wrong about [bad people] all
these thousands of years. Flogging and bread-and-water, you
know, and Holy Communion, when what they really needed
was a little bit of rabbit-gland or something to make them just

as good as gold."[60] Sayers expects us to laugh at this muddled behaviorist, but I suspect it would be wiser to recoil in fear.

Once a person believes that they "know what's best" for mankind, it's easy for them to administer treatment even if it makes the patient gag. If a person knows the way to improve society to help men redeem themselves, then he is justified in behaving like a skilled doctor treating a cancer patient. The doctor may prescribe radiation therapy, which will cause the patient a lot of suffering—but the patient must trust the doctor, believing that the short-term suffering will be worth the long-term recovery. In the same way, the man who can fix society wants to give us the rabbit-gland or the Goals 2000 or the Social Security even if it makes many people suffer. Supposedly, he's the "expert" who can make everything right.

But this reliance on different plans and ideologies as medications that will make men better has only made things worse. Solzhenitsyn knows:

> Ideology—that is what gives evildoing its long-sought justification and gives the evildoer the necessary steadfastness and determination. That is the social theory which helps to make his acts seem good instead of bad in his own and others' eyes, so that he won't hear reproaches and curses but will receive praise and honors. That was how the agents of the Inquisition fortified their wills: by invoking Christianity; the conquerors of foreign lands, by extolling the grandeur of their Motherland; the colonizers, by civilization; the Nazis, by race; and the Jacobins (early and late), by

equality, brotherhood, and the happiness of
future generations.

Thanks to *ideology*, the twentieth century
was fated to experience evildoing on a scale
calculated in the millions. This cannot be
denied, nor passed over, nor suppressed.[61]

The Frankenstein crowd is always in danger of obsessing with a
new ideology or a new plan to save the world—and in the
process, trampling individuals. The Hyde crowd should always
value individuals more than civilizations. At best, non-Christians hope to see Cuba's government changed; Christians want
to see even a murderer like Fidel Castro changed. It's ironic, of
course: the very people who think that men are capable of all
kinds of horrendous evils—who actually expect men to kill and
lie and cheat and steal—value the individual far more than
those who claim that he is basically good. If you begin with
Frankenstein, only the self and society matter; if you begin
with Hyde, *everyone* matters.

In *Lord of the Flies*, the chief of the tribe of little boys
marooned on the island "wanted to explain how people were
never quite what you thought they were."[62] The Frankenstein
crowd needs to learn this lesson. No social scheme can "free"
man to save himself, because no man—even the best and the
brightest—is quite what we hope he is. As the children on that
island discovered, societies based on man-centered values
descend into tyranny and barbarism.

If men hope to live in a society that promotes liberty and
justice, their nation must acknowledge the sovereignty of God.
But even such national obedience cannot guarantee freedom
on earth. Freedom, according to the Christian worldview, is

not a property of nations or locations, and it thrives in the strangest places, including prison camps and sweatshops and plantations. Freedom grows everywhere, in the hearts of men and women who have surrendered their lives to Christ and by His power become slaves to righteousness.

"[B]eing good is an adventure far more violent and
daring than sailing round the world."[1]
—Basil Grant,
a character invented by G.K. Chesterton

CHAPTER 6

A MONSTROUS PARADOX

Mary Shelley conceived the story of Frankenstein when she was still a teenager, as a response to a challenge from her husband, Percy Bysshe Shelley, and another famous Romantic poet, Lord Byron. Like the Shelleys, Lord Byron believed in the monster of Frankenstein—that is, he trusted that man was basically good—and he carried this faith to his deathbed.

According to tradition, Byron's last words were a question and a defiant answer: "Shall I sue for mercy? Come, come, no weakness. Let me be a man to the last."[2] This final cry is the cry of every non-Christian.

Should man sue for mercy? The non-Christian must respond with a resounding *no*. If man is basically good, he shouldn't require mercy from God or nature or any other source—instead he should pull himself up by his bootstraps and keep the Ten Commandments or deny the existence of suffering or do whatever it takes to rescue himself. To grovel for mercy would be a failure to esteem his own capabilities.

The Hyde crowd responds by asking non-Christians to look around them. Man's attempts to save himself, via psychology or his own hard work, leave him still riddled with guilt and buffeted by suffering. His attempts to improve society via government leave men unredeemed in a society that is less just and less free. Should man sue for mercy? The question is best answered by another question: What else can he do?

Byron believed that by refusing God's mercy he remained a "man to the last." He was right. The tragedy is that he had the chance to be much, much more than a man.

In 1 Corinthians 3:2-3, Paul chastises Christians in Corinth for their immaturity: "I gave you milk, not solid food, for you were not yet ready for it. Indeed, you are still not ready. You are still worldly. For since there is jealousy and quarreling among you, are you not worldly? Are you not acting like mere men?" Strange words, when you consider that the people in Corinth were not aliens or angels or titans. They were men. So why does Paul chastise them for behaving that way?

The answer should take our breath away: Christians are men and women set free from sin by virtue of the fact that the Holy Spirit dwells within them. We are not "mere men," but instead the Body of Christ—and as part of that Body we should live as differently as our worldview differs from every other.

G.K. Chesterton also had something to say on his death-bed, and his last words remind us that Christianity is nothing like any other faith: "The issue now is clear: it is between light and darkness and everyone must choose his side."[3] Christianity differs radically from every other worldview with regard to our beliefs about the nature of man, the nature of God, ethics, self-esteem, guilt, suffering, government, family, and church—who, then, would expect Christians to behave like non-Christians? We should instead stand out like lanterns in the blackest forest, as different from men as Martians.

Of course, it doesn't work like that for me very often—you would have to look awfully closely at my life to see a change.

If I'm a lantern in a forest, I'm a dark lantern that too often keeps the panel closed. And you might feel the same way—often indistinguishable from the non-Christian. You might ask whether it is realistic to expect us to behave otherwise.

But you've got to consider the Source. It's not just some writer or some apostle telling us to stop acting like a mere man or woman. God Himself—the God Who understands the depths of our sinfulness far more than we understand—expects us to behave radically differently (by the power of the Holy Spirit). We may think this sounds impossible or unrealistic; we may protest that we've really tried to change and we're lousy at it; we may complain that we are weaker than the martyrs and heroes of the Christian faith. It doesn't matter. We may say we can't; God says we can: "Therefore, if anyone is in Christ, he is a new creation; the old has gone, the new has come!" (2 Corinthians 5:17). And this new creation is expected to *live like Christ lived*—humbly, mercifully, righteously, perfectly.

"There is nothing in the annals of history to match that particular personality," says William Kilpatrick. "Next to it, the psychological models of health and wholeness are dust and nonsense."[4] And yet somehow Christians are supposed to emulate Christ's perfection.

Christians won't achieve perfection until heaven, of course, but it bears remembering that each of us is destined to make it one day. C.S. Lewis says that God uses our time on earth to move us in that direction: "[N]o possible degree of holiness or heroism which has ever been recorded of the greatest saints is beyond what He is determined to produce in every one of us in the end. The job will not be completed in this life: but He means to get us *as far as possible* before death."[5] We won't be perfect here and now, but we should be showing some signs of righteousness—and these signs will make us stick out like imperfect sculptures in a sea of clay. Christians won't be perfect, but we should look quite different as we take shape under the hands of the Master. "Until you have given up your self to Him," writes Lewis, "you will not have a real self. Sameness is to be found most among the most 'natural' men, not among those who surrender to Christ. How monotonously alike all the great tyrants and conquerors have been: how gloriously different are the saints."[6]

Karl Barth defines *wisdom* as "the knowledge by which we may actually and practically live."[7] Christians have this; non-Christians don't. A non-Christian may possess whole storehouses of knowledge—he may know the best way to build a bridge, the best way to fix a car, and the entire history of philosophy—but he cannot have wisdom. While non-Christians follow Buddha or Mohammed or Joseph Smith and their own selfish desires, Christians follow the Way, the Truth, and the Life. All other ways lead to pettiness; only Christ calls men to perfection.

And so we arrive at last at the biggest paradox: Christians, the very people who claim that man can do nothing to save himself, expect more goodness of themselves than any other adherent of any other worldview. "Christianity is strange," writes Blaise Pascal. "It bids man to recognize that he is vile, and even abominable, and bids him want to be like God."[8] While the Frankenstein crowd searches frantically for a way to save themselves, the Hyde crowd "sues for mercy" and then finds themselves free from sin and called to Christ-likeness. The irony is profound: men who deny their sinfulness and posture as gods-in-the-making stay "mere men," while men who acknowledge their sinfulness become, by Christ's power, sons of God! "For whoever wants to save his life will lose it, but whoever loses his life for me will save it" (Luke 9:24). Broken vessels can only be used when they recognize that they can accomplish nothing on their own—then suddenly these broken vessels find that they are expected not only to live well, but to be holy. "Man," as Chesterton says, "is not merely an evolution but rather a revolution"[9]—a being called from death to life, from blindness to sight, and from sin to heroism.

THE HEROIC LIFE

Please understand: this is not hyperbole. *Heroism* is a big word, I know, and it conjures images of firemen rushing into burning buildings and mothers quietly going hungry so that their children can eat. We think of heroes as people in stories or on television, not real people in our neighborhood—and certainly not us! But thinking this way requires dismissing the Sermon on the Mount and just about everything else Christ said. What could be more heroic than turning the other cheek or going the extra mile or surrendering all that you have or loving your enemy? Make no mistake, the Christian is called to lead a heroic life. "The path for the followers of Christ," says Russell Kirk, "was a stonier road than ever men had been told to follow before. Its principles demanded a new sort of heroism, more severe than that of the Law of the Jews, more sacrificing of self than the old Roman virtue."[10]

The world cannot account for heroism. Properly understood, heroism is synonymous with selflessness—and the world calls only for selfishness. When a man dives in an icy river to save an octogenarian, he has only two possible motives: helping himself or helping his fellow man. If saving the elderly person

235

means collecting a reward—be it money or eternal salvation—
the "hero's" motive is merely selfish. Only the man who risks
his life *selflessly*—not for money or power or glory but only
because he loves his neighbor—can truly be called a hero.
Every other worldview says we should help others because in
the long run it will help us. Only Christ provides salvation
first, and then demands that we die to ourselves every day.

As always, B.F. Skinner understood the implications of his
denial that man is sinful. He describes his perfect society as "a
world without heroes,"[11] because no one can be heroic in a
world where no one has free will. Other non-Christians less
consistent than Skinner disagree with him, of course, and
many are willing to acknowledge the rather obvious fact that
men occasionally behave heroically. But these non-Christians
must redefine heroism to make it fit their worldview. At the
very best, non-Christians can only view heroism as dramatic
acts of selfishness that also happen to benefit others. Such a
definition pales in the face of men like Dietrich Bonhoeffer.

In the 1930s and '40s, Bonhoeffer and his German coun-
trymen watched Adolf Hitler accumulate power and escalate
persecution. At first, Hitler's government simply requested
that Christian churches register with the state. Later Hitler
demanded it, closing the doors of churches that refused. In an
effort to regulate church doctrine, Hitler established an official
Nazi church, the German Reich Church. Seminary candidates
for this church were required to prove that they had pure
Aryan blood and to swear allegiance to the Nazi party. Hitler
even replaced the cross above the altar in some churches with a
stylized cross-and-swastika.

Tragically, many German Christians meekly complied with
Hitler's adulteration of their faith. But Bonhoeffer could not.

Bonhoeffer understood that Christ called him to follow Him regardless of the danger or the personal cost. "To deny oneself," writes Bonhoeffer, "is to be aware only of Christ and no more of self, to see only him who goes before and no more the road which is too hard for us. Once more, all self-denial can say is: 'He leads the way, keep close to him.'"[12] To obey Christ meant disobeying Hitler, which was dangerous, but biblical precedent required it (Daniel 6:6-10, Acts 4:18-19).

So in 1935, Bonhoeffer established an underground seminary to help train pastors to teach the Word of God. The Gestapo discovered this seminary and closed it down, imprisoning 27 former students. Though Bonhoeffer had already caused the Nazis enough consternation that they forbade him to lecture at the University of Berlin and later forbade him from printing or publishing, he chose to serve as a double agent in the *Abwehr*—Hitler's military intelligence organization—so that he could more effectively aid the persecuted. In 1941, Bonhoeffer's spy work led him to become involved in "Operation 7," a rescue mission that saved Jews by smuggling them across the German border into Switzerland. Instead of rolling over and watching Hitler pervert Christianity, Bonhoeffer stood fast.

This obedience would ultimately cost Bonhoeffer everything. In 1943, the same year he became engaged, he was arrested and imprisoned in Tegel Prison. After spending more than two years in one of Hitler's infamous prison camps, Bonhoeffer was hanged for treason. The same month Adolf Hitler committed suicide.

Dietrich Bonhoeffer never called himself a hero, but his life was heroic. In an effort to follow Christ—not to ensure his salvation, not to garner earthly rewards—Bonhoeffer sacrificed his career, his future marriage, his friends and his life. Not by his power, but by the power of the Holy Spirit, Bonhoeffer walked the narrow path. Though he would never admit it, his words describe his life: "To be called to a life of extraordinary quality, to live up to it, and yet to be unconscious of it is indeed a narrow way."[13]

The world is quick to remind Christians of all the ways that Christians fail. Non-Christians love to discuss Jim and Tammy Faye, corrupt popes, and the racism of various pastors, because these failures suggest that Christians are hypocrites. Isn't Christ supposed to transform lives? Then why do so many Christians sin so often?

Christians experience these same doubts. If I have the Holy Spirit living within me, and I have been set free from sin, why do I sin all the time? Why don't I shine brighter in a dark world? I don't need non-Christians to tell me that Christians can be hypocritical—I see it in the mirror every day. The failures of Christians are painfully obvious both in the world and in my life.

Often the tendency when faced with these failures is to turn away, in the hopes that we can protect ourselves from discouragement. But this willful ignorance is unwise. Acknowledging failures isn't bad—in fact, Christians *should* remember that they often fall short of God's standard. Our proper attitude toward God is one of humility, understanding that all good things come from Him. The only times we really are out of touch with reality are those times when we think, like the Pharisees, that we are doing "pretty good" at being righteous. When we recognize our neediness and our failings, we recognize our need to rely completely on Christ.

Consequently, I consider it a favor when non-Christians remind me that Christians aren't perfect—but I also seek to remind them (and myself) of another historical fact: Christians often lead heroic lives. Just as Christians must remember their failures, they must also remember their victories—both corporately and individually. The antidote to discouragement is not blinding our eyes to our sin, but opening our eyes to the transforming power of the Holy Spirit in people's lives. While we remember the Jim and Tammy Fayes, we must also remember the Bonhoeffers, understanding that the Holy Spirit can change us as radically as that thorn in Hitler's side. We must, as Sir Thomas Browne advises, keep our eyes fixed on the heroes:

> And therefore though vicious times invert the opinions of things, and set up a new Ethicks against Virtue, yet hold thou unto old Morality; and rather than follow a multitude to do evil, stand like *Pompey's* pillar conspicuous by thyself, and single in Integrity. And . . . since no Deluge of Vice is like to be so general but more than eight will escape; Eye well those Heroes who have held their Heads above Water, who have touched Pitch, and not been defiled, and in the common Contagion have remained uncorrupted.[14]

Christians should focus on heroes not for the purpose of hero-worship, but simply to remind themselves that the Holy Spirit wants to do the same thing with their own lives. Though it's easy to distance myself from Bonhoeffer because

his actions far surpass my own, I must instead remember that
Bonhoeffer accomplished nothing by himself. He and I are
equally incapable of doing good—and he and I share in
common the one Hope for doing good, the Holy Spirit.

When you think of the Body of Christ, the tendency is to
picture Charles Colson as the eyes and Franklin Graham as the
mouth and yourself as the big toe or the armpit. We think that
better men may achieve great things by the grace of God, but
that we are lucky to just get by. Such an attitude is unbiblical.
There are no *better* men, only men who have made themselves
more available to be used by God. As Joel Belz likes to say,
every one of us is the lost sheep in the parable of the sheep
(Matthew 18:10-14). The 99 "found" sheep are merely literary
props—they don't exist. Each of us was a sinner hopelessly
dead in our sins; each of us was sought by the Shepherd and
rescued; each of us now has the opportunity to follow Him.
That's all heroism is: getting out of the way and letting God
lead.

George Roche says it best: "[W]e are all asked to be heroes,
each in his own circumstances. We are misled by our perspective. In seeing the heroic as too large for ourselves, we have
been deceived and cheated by man-made philosophies that see
human purpose as far too small."[15] Our purpose is none other
than to glorify God, and every Christian has been set free to do
exactly that.

Naturally we don't like to think that God expects *us* to be
heroic, because it means a lot more work; it means dying to
ourselves and letting God be in control; it means being un-
comfortable and sometimes even persecuted. "Every man,"
writes Alexander Solzhenitsyn, "always has handy a dozen glib

little reasons why he is right not to sacrifice himself."[16] And each of these excuses comes from the flesh. When we listen instead to God, we will find that He is calling us to sacrifice everything.

CHARACTER EDUCATION

Non-Christians love to be in charge of education. Since they believe they know what man must do to save himself, they want to pass this knowledge on to the next generation as quickly and efficiently as possible. It makes sense. If man is going to redeem himself, he'd better learn the best methods from the best teachers.

Christians should also love education. Scripture tells us that if we "train a child in the way he should go," then "when he is old he will not turn from it" (Proverbs 22:6). We understand that God honors parents' efforts to raise their children to please Him. But unfortunately Christians often ignore the most important component of education: teaching by example.

The world begins education at the same place it begins everything: with the assumption that man is basically good. Kilpatrick examined various public school curriculums and concluded that the curriculum writers "assume a sort of natural goodness and integrity in the child, whereby he or she will always want to do the right thing."[17] Elsewhere he notes that "The common feature they all share is the assumption that children can learn to make good moral decisions without bothering to acquire moral habits or strength of character."[18] Christians, on the other hand, recognize that goodness doesn't come naturally and that teaching people to behave morally is a difficult task. Nothing the teacher does can make a student actually good; it's hard enough to encourage someone to be outwardly moral.

The best way to encourage morality is not to free students to get in touch with themselves—their tendency is toward sin. Instead, the best way to encourage morality is to *model* it.[19] Do we want people to understand what it means to be born again? Well, we can talk about it until we've bored them straight into a coma, but we won't have explained it to them until we've lived it. Actions speak louder—and more eloquently—than words. The warning in 1 John 3:18 rings true: "Dear children, let us not love with words or tongue but with actions and in truth." The heroism of Bonhoeffer is worth a thousand words.

Great authors have understood this throughout the ages. How does one express the inexpressible? How can you teach the deepest truths? Not through syllogisms or essays, but through *stories*. Bare words can only explain so much; actions describe much more. We learn more about courage by reading about Atticus Finch than by reading a thousand dictionaries' definitions of courage.

We learn even more if we live in the cell next to Bonhoeffer. Any story can be a great teaching tool, but true stories are the best. We may certainly teach people about God's grace by telling them the story of *Pilgrim's Progress*; we teach it better when we tell them the true story of John New-ton; and we teach it best when we demonstrate it with our own lives. Our actions matter more than any words, even stories.

It is my hope that your journey through this book has galvanized your desire to see people reject the Frankenstein myth and embrace Christ. If I've accomplished what I set out to do, you're anxious to teach others the truth of the Christian worldview. How can you do this? By example! Your words matter, but not nearly as much as your life matters. In order to be best used by the Holy Spirit, you must model truth for the rest of the world. Only when non-Christians see Christ manifest in His Body will they, like Dr. Jekyll, see "the veil of self-indulgence . . . rent from head to foot."[20] You (and I) must exemplify the fact that Christ changes lives—and this means leading heroic lives.

Properly understood, following Christ is an adventure story. Once upon a time, the King put on the clothes of a beggar and walked among us. Although the King was discovered and killed, He conquered death and set His people free. Today He sits on the throne and the war is won, but the question still remains: Who will follow Him? Who will serve as His eyes, ears, feet and hands, and demonstrate His rule to a fallen world? Who will take the challenge to obey His orders, even when it means risking family, friends, possessions, and our own life?

You may not feel that you have been called to face the next Hitler or start an underground seminary or lead the fight against abortion—and you may be right. Perhaps you were never meant to be a front-line hero remembered throughout history. Perhaps no one in the twenty-second century will know your name. But you are called to a heroic, adventurous life nonetheless. Kilpatrick explains:

> [W]e come to realize that there are more
> ordinary kinds of heroism, from which daring
> deeds . . . are absent, which are for the most
> part unsung and unrecorded, but which
> nevertheless require great endurance and

ingenuity. This adventure will take the form of a journey, but it will most likely be an interior journey. There will be a desire to tell the story, but the audience for it will be small: perhaps only one or two others will know, perhaps only God. The most common form this adventure takes is marrying and raising a family— although there are certainly other forms.[21]

Elsewhere he says, "The heroic thing required of ordinary people is sustained commitment."[22] Such commitment will necessarily demand hard work and sacrifice—the very backbone of adventure.

The beauty of the adventurous life, as C.E.M. Joad understands, is that it teaches us to appreciate all that God provides:

I have come, that is to say, to see life in terms of a challenge, a challenge to effort and endeavour, a challenge to sacrifice and self-denial. . . . I have found by experience that unless the effort and endeavour have been expended, the pleasures of tranquil enjoyment cannot be tasted. The pot of tea and the anchovy toast, the boiled egg and the home-made strawberry jam, never taste so well, the enjoyment of the armchair by the blazing fire is never so consciously savoured as after a day's climb in the hills in sleet and mist.[23]

Put simply, we never rest so comfortably in God's hands until we exhaust ourselves following Him.

If we adventure well, people will notice. We may never make the front page of *USA Today* or the index in a history textbook, but our neighbors and our families will see the excitement inherent in the Christian life. Those close to you can learn, by watching the story of your life, the plain truth that believing in Frankenstein leads to despair and selfishness, while believing in Hyde leads to adventure and joy. "Perhaps the best comment that one can make," writes Kilpatrick, "is to repeat G.K. Chesterton's remark that 'it is only too easy to forget that there is a thrill in theism.' But where, we must ask in all seriousness, is the thrill in me-ism?"[24] Your friends are reminded of the thrill in Christianity when they see you living heroically by the power of the Holy Spirit.

And in some cases, as with Gene Stallings, people quietly going about the business of following Christ can cause millions to take notice. Stallings was the football coach at the University of Alabama, but he didn't use that position to noisily draw attention to his commitment to Christ. Instead, he simply backed up his commitment with his life—and consequently his life was so different that the world was startled. In a recent issue of *The Sporting News*, a feature article began with the story of a wife and husband, Debbie and Gary Oliver, badly injured in an auto accident. In a hospital far from home, the wife was confined to a wheelchair and the husband lay in a coma. Oddly enough, a strange man started visiting Gary almost every day. When Debbie finally bumped into the visitor, he introduced himself as—you guessed it—Gene Stallings. When her husband recovered from his coma two months later, Gary told Debbie that he could remember only one voice from his ordeal: the voice of Gene Stallings. *The Sporting News* ends the story this way:

> "Why did [Stallings] do it?" Debbie Oliver asks. There is a long silence before she says softly, "Because he is Christ-like. This is what Christ would do. It is the true meaning of Christianity. To go out of his way to help. He is a busy man. But this was genuine."[25]

Christians don't have to demand respect for our worldview or nag the world to notice our beliefs. If we live what we believe, the world is compelled to pay attention! Quiet selflessness on the part of Stallings represented the truth of Christianity better than a thousand post-game lectures about his faith.[26]

Of course, not everyone in the Frankenstein crowd is willing to do what *The Sporting News* did. Many non-Christians would rather pretend that they don't notice Christians leading transformed lives, because they don't appreciate being reminded that Christianity is true. As Christ warns, those in darkness hate the light (John 3:19-20). When Alexander Ogorodnikov was arrested (again) by the KGB for obeying Christ rather than the leaders of the Soviet Union, the KGB agent told him, "We understand you want very much to be a hero. But we don't want to make new martyrs."[27] Why not? Because heroism undermines the lie that Christ is not our Savior!

When you live consistently with your faith, many non-Christians will feel threatened. Lies are comfortable, and many would rather have comfort than the truth. A certain abortionist provides us with a classic example . . .

Christians witnessing on the sidewalk outside this abortionist's clinic were hitting a little too close to home: in a year, they convinced six of his employees to quit their jobs at the clinic. These Christians found new jobs for each of the former employees, and led three of them to trust Christ! In desperation, the abortionist created a contract that he requires his new employees to sign. It reads:

> Please note that any contact between staff employees of A CHOICE FOR WOMEN [the abortion clinic] and members of OPERA-TION RESCUE [the Christians] will not be tolerated during office hours. Contact after hours is considered immorale [sic]. In either case any such contact may result in termination of the employment.[28]

Could you ever, in your wildest dreams, imagine a better advertisement for Christianity? According to this abortionist, Christianity is so appealing that rational adults who support abortion can be snatched away by simply talking to Christians! Employees of a clinic called "A Choice for Women" are forbidden to choose to talk to Christians because the Christian choice is too compelling!

Other non-Christians advertise the truth of Christianity in other ways. My favorite advertisement was provided by authorities in the Catholic Church in 1428, who dug up the body of John Wycliffe forty years after he had died, burned his bones, and threw his ashes into the Swift River. Apparently Wycliffe, a Christian whose life laid the foundation for the Reformation, was such a threat to heresy that he had to be killed again!

The Invisible Man

Consider the distance we have traveled. The Hyde crowd begins with the bad news that man is sinful through and through, and ends by expecting God to cause Christians to live heroically. Non-Christians begin with the "good news" of the monster of Frankenstein, and end by creating another monster: the Invisible Man.

In *The Invisible Man*, H.G. Wells describes yet another "mad scientist" who created a monster. The scientist, Dr. Griffin, discovers the process by which he can become invisible—which seems to give him a profound advantage over his fellow man. But the advantage is illusory; in truth, invisibility proves to be a curse that sentences the Invisible Man to a life of being trampled on, run into, and despised by society. He cannot hide, because he still makes noises. He cannot wear clothes, because the clothes are still visible. If he sheds his clothes, he freezes in the January cold of England. The reader recognizes that the Invisible Man is trapped in a downward spiral: he selfishly sought invisibility for his own gain, and now his invisibility forces him to become more and more selfish. Soon his every thought is centered on keeping his existence comfortable and ensuring that he receives everything he thinks he deserves. In the end the Invisible Man becomes, according to one of his closest confidants, "pure selfishness. He thinks of nothing but his own advantage . . ."[29]

The Frankenstein crowd must end in the same place. Though non-Christians believe that they know how man can save himself—whether by obeying the Word of Wisdom or following the Four Noble Truths or building utopia—they are out of touch with reality, and so their experiments go awry. As non-Christians discover that life is not everything they hoped it would be—they are trampled on and they suffer—their own selfish desires become more and more important to them. In the end, the non-Christian thinks of nothing but his own advantage: how he can redeem himself and become happy. Like the invisible man, he can only wreak havoc in a quest for personal gain.

The non-Christian flirts daily with a hollow, chaotic life, as Barth warns:

> Whenever man, no matter in what dimension or by what title, tries to present himself and act as his own redeemer and that of his environment—whether in seizing or expanding external power, or in living out his sexuality, or in acquiring and increasing his material possessions, or as the maker of a new universe of his own on the authority of his own inner convictions, or in the development and putting into practice of a political, technological or economic theory or ideology, or as a thinking individual who engages in abstract, professorial thought—in practice he ends up under the wheels. He may perhaps become 'civilized,' but he will surely be dehumanized, i.e. alienated from himself and his fellow-men, changed from a free man to a slave of the spirits he has conjured up like the sorcerer's apprentice and let loose against himself and the world about him. Then he is at the mercy of all the utterly irrational supreme beings, absolutes, gods and

sovereigns, their arbitrary will and their conflict. That is the beginning of the chaos, and
of that one can well be afraid.[30]

It's no use saying that any worldview is as good as any other
worldview. Christianity differs dramatically from every other
worldview, and as a result it demands dramatically different
behavior from its adherents. When a person is asked to
choose, it seems wise for that person to side with the
worldview that leads to heroism instead of chaos.

"It is rather ridiculous," says Chesterton, "to ask a man just
about to be boiled in a pot and eaten, at a purely religious
feast, why he does not regard all religions as equally friendly
and fraternal."[31] They are not. Christianity leads to selflessness, while the rest lead only to a nondescript selfishness.
"Only the selfless man lives responsibly," says Bonhoeffer, "and
this means that only the selfless man *lives*."[32] The more often
Christians demonstrate this truth, the more difficult it will be
for the world to ignore.

Should we sue for mercy? Not if we want to remain "mere
men." But if we want to become sons of God, we must. Only
Christ offers life, and life abundantly. The man who trusts
Christ receives not only eternal life, but also—if he is willing to
pick up his cross—a life filled with excitement and adventure.
If we allow the Holy Spirit to guide us on this adventure, God
can use our lives to help others escape the deadliest monster.

J.F. BALDWIN

NOTES

PROLOGUE

1. Robert Louis Stevenson, *Dr. Jekyll and Mr. Hyde* (New York, NY: Bantam, 1981), p. 78.
2. Ibid, p. 18.
3. Ibid, p. 24.
4. Ibid, p. 34.
5. Ibid, p. 79.
6. Mary Shelley, *Frankenstein* (New York, NY: Bantam, 1981), p. 104.
7. Ibid, p. 126.
8. Ibid, p. 131.

CHAPTER 1

1. Blaise Pascal, *Pensees* (New York, NY: Penguin, 1986), p. 245.
2. Mary Shelley, *Frankenstein* (New York, NY: Bantam, 1981), p. 84.
3. Robert Louis Stevenson, *Dr. Jekyll and Mr. Hyde* (New York, NY: Bantam, 1981), p. 80.
4. Shelley, *Frankenstein*, p. 204.
5. Stevenson, *Dr. Jekyll and Mr. Hyde*, p. 85.
6. G.K. Chesterton, *Robert Louis Stevenson* (New York, NY: Dodd, Mead & Co., 1928), p. 199.
7. Plato, *Phaedrus* (New York, NY: Penguin, 1995), p. 29.
8. Strictly speaking, natural man is all Hyde and no Jekyll—that is, before we are redeemed we are completely dead in our sins and cannot intend or do good (by our own power) even for a moment. While the story of Jekyll and Hyde doesn't perfectly match reality for natural man, it closely matches his experience. It seems to unredeemed man that he can sometimes do good (when he chooses to control his temper rather than hit someone, for example). Though natural man is totally depraved, he believes himself to be a mixture of good and bad.
9. Some might object that Paul tells Christians to "work out your salvation" in Philippians 2:12, but this verse takes on an entirely different meaning in context. In verse 13 Paul explains that "*it is God who works in you* to will and to act according to his good purpose" (emphasis added).
10. Carl Rogers, "Notes on Rollo May," *Journal of Humanistic Psychology*, Summer 1982, p. 8.

11. Abraham Maslow, cited in *Humanistic Psychology*, eds. I. David Welch, George A. Tate, and Fred Richards (Buffalo, NY: Prometheus, 1978), p. 190.
12. Aldous Huxley, *The Perennial Philosophy* (New York, NY: Harper & Row, 1970), p. 14.
13. *Humanist Manifesto II* (Buffalo, NY: Prometheus, 1973), p. 16.
14. To say that you can't be sure about whether or not God exists (as agnostics do) is to believe quite a few things about the nature of God. For example, the agnostic's beliefs imply that even if God does exist He is incompetent at revealing Himself, or has deserted mankind—and therefore mankind cannot be held responsible for any rebellion against that Being.
15. Barbara von der Heydt, *Candles Behind the Wall* (Grand Rapids, MI: Eerdmans, 1993), p. xvii.
16. Thomas H. Huxley invented the term *agnostic* because he wanted a socially acceptable word for atheist. He sought to change the terms of the origins debate so that science became mankind's only certain method for obtaining knowledge, and then he sought to exclude Christianity from scientific discussions. While lecturing the Young Men's Christian Association, he proclaimed that the sciences are "neither Christian, nor Unchristian, but are Extra-christian . . ." according to Adrian Desmond, *Huxley: The Devil's Disciple* (London: Michael Joseph, 1994), p. 374.
17. B.F. Skinner, *Beyond Freedom and Dignity* (New York, NY: Bantam, 1972), p. 63.
18. Erich Fromm, *You Shall Be as Gods* (New York, NY: Holt, Rinehart and Winston, 1966), p. 23.
19. Rumors abound that Darwin repented and was born again shortly before he died. Although no one knows for certain, the best available evidence suggests that these rumors have little truth to them. For a discussion of this possibility, see Ian Taylor, *In the Minds of Men* (Toronto: TFE, 1991), pp. 136-7.
20. For a more extensive critique of Buddhism, see Stephen Neill, *Christian Faith and Other Faiths* (Downers Grove, IL: InterVarsity, 1984).
21. Neill also provides a good critique of Hinduism in *Christian Faith and Other Faiths*. For a more general critique of pantheism, see chapter seven of James Sire, *The Universe Next Door* (Downers Grove, IL: InterVarsity, 1988).
22. For a more extensive critique of Islam, see William Miller, *A Christian's Response to Islam* (Phillipsburg, NJ: Presbyterian and Reformed, 1976).

23. Hammudah Abdalati, *Islam in Focus* (Indianapolis, IN: American Trust, 1977), p. 33.
24. Ibid, p. 32.
25. Ibid.
26. *Insight on the Scriptures* (Brooklyn, NY: Watchtower Bible and Tract Society, 1988), vol. 2, p. 792.
27. "You Can Live Forever in Paradise on Earth—But How?" *The Watchtower*, February 15, 1983, pp. 12-13.
28. David J. Goldberg and John D. Rayner, *The Jewish People: Their History and Their Religion* (New York, NY: Viking Penguin, 1987), p. 264. Although Goldberg and Rayner are not the most orthodox of Jews, their statements accurately reflect the traditional Jewish position.
29. David J. Wolpe, *Teaching Your Children About God* (New York, NY: Henry Holt & Co., 1993), p. 137.
30. David S. Ariel, *What Do Jews Believe?* (New York, NY: Shocken, 1995), p. 91.
31. Ibid, pp. 84-85.
32. One of the Mormon Sunday school books states clearly that "We can become Gods like our Heavenly Father. This is exaltation." *Gospel Principles* (Salt Lake City, UT: The Church of Jesus Christ of Latter-day Saints, 1979), p. 290.
33. M. Russell Ballard, *Our Search for Happiness* (Salt Lake City, UT: Deseret, 1993), p. 87.
34. Ibid, p. 12.
35. *Gospel Principles*, p. 285.
36. Ibid, p. 292.
37. The best example of this New Age obsession with casting off all authority is their willingness to treat all sacred scriptures as largely irrelevant: "We can take all the scriptures, and all the teachings, and all the tablets, and all the laws, and all the marshmallows and have a jolly good bonfire and marshmallow roast, because that is all they are worth." David Spangler, *Reflections on the Christ* (Scotland: Findhorn, 1982), p. 73.
38. Marianne Williamson, *A Return to Love* (New York, NY: HarperCollins, 1992), p. 257.
39. M. Scott Peck, *People of the Lie* (New York, NY: Simon & Schuster, 1983), p. 11.
40. Shirley MacLaine, *It's All in the Playing* (New York, NY: Bantam, 1987), pp. 173-174.
41. Gloria Steinem, *Revolution from Within* (Boston, MA: Little, Brown & Co., 1992), p. 156.

42. Ibid, p. 153.
43. C.S. Lewis, *The Screwtape Letters* (New York, NY: Macmillan, 1982), p. 43. Incredibly, the senior demon is deceitful even when he instructs his junior. He implies that some men don't have a religion, but in truth every thinking person has a religion or a worldview, as we shall see in chapter two.
44. William Kirk Kilpatrick, *Psychological Seduction* (Nashville, TN: Thomas Nelson, 1983), p. 146.
45. Karl Barth, "Atheism, For and Against," *Fragments Grave and Gay* (Glasgow: William Collins Sons, 1976), pp. 46-47.
46. Dorothy Sayers, "Creed or Chaos," *The Whimsical Christian* (New York, NY: Macmillan, 1987), p. 42.
47. Leo Booth, *When God Becomes a Drug* (Los Angeles, CA: Jeremy P. Tarcher, 1991), p. 38.
48. Anthony A. Hoekema, *The Christian Looks at Himself* (Grand Rapids, MI: Eerdmans, 1975), p. 17.
49. Kilpatrick, *Psychological Seduction,* p. 39.
50. Ibid, p. 83.
51. Robert Louis Stevenson, "Pulvis et Umbra," *Across the Plains* (New York, NY: Charles Scribner's Sons, 1899), pp. 294-298.
52. Alexander Solzhenitsyn, *The Gulag Archipelago* (New York, NY: Harper & Row, 1974), p. 168.
53. Viktor Frankl, *Man's Search for Meaning* (New York, NY: Washington Square Press, 1963), pp. 213-214.
54. Pascal, *Pensees,* p. 64.
55. Bruno Bettelheim, *The Uses of Enchantment: The Meaning and Importance of Fairy Tales* (New York, NY: Knopf, 1976), p. 7.
56. Pascal, *Pensees,* p. 65.
57. Ibid, p. 154.
58. Kilpatrick, *Psychological Seduction,* p. 104.
59. G.K. Chesterton, *The Club of Queer Trades* (New York, NY: Penguin, 1984), p. 10.
60. Fyodor Dostoevsky, *Notes from the Underground* in *Three Short Novels of Dostoevsky* (Garden City, NY: Doubleday & Co., 1960), p.297.
61. Pascal, *Pensees,* p. 229.
62. C.S. Lewis, *Beyond Personality* (New York, NY: Macmillan, 1947), p. 36.
63. Kilpatrick, *Psychological Seduction,* p. 71.
64. Pascal, *Pensees,* p. 297.
65. Ibid, p. 42.
66. C.S. Lewis, "Good Work and Good Works," *The World's Last Night* (San Diego, CA: Harcourt Brace, 1987), p. 77.

67. John Vasconcellos, "Preface," *The Social Importance of Self-Esteem,* eds. Andrew M. Mecca, Neil J. Smelser, and John Vasconcellos (Berkeley, CA: University of California, 1989), p. xii.

68. James J.D. Luce, "The Fundamentalists Anonymous Movement," *The Humanist,* Jan/Feb 1986, p. 11.

69. G.K. Chesterton, *The Everlasting Man* (Garden City, NY: Doubleday & Co., 1955), p. 164.

70. Charles Colson, *Loving God* (Grand Rapids, MI: Zondervan, 1987), p. 120.

CHAPTER 2

1. Abraham Lincoln, October 16, 1854, *A Treasury of Lincoln Quotations,* ed. Fred Kerner (Garden City, NY: Doubleday & Co., 1965), p. 134.

2. Blaise Pascal, *Pensees* (New York, NY: Penguin, 1986), p. 64.

3. G.K. Chesterton, *The Everlasting Man* (Garden City, NY: Doubleday, 1955), p. 15.

4. In itself, this is a good argument for the inappropriateness of state schools. Parents, and not government officials, should determine the worldview that most influences their children's education. Today far too many parents see that decision made for them by administrators in the school district in which they happen to live.

5. This alternative to the modern myth of separation was recommended as the "non-preferentialist" perspective by Supreme Court Justice William Rhenquist in Mueller v. Allen (1993).

6. Charles J. McFadden, *The Philosophy of Communism* (New York, NY: Benziger Brothers, 1963), p. 298.

7. Even reliance upon reason requires faith. "It is idle to talk always of the alternative of reason and faith," says Chesterton. "Reason is itself a matter of faith. It is an act of faith to assert that our thoughts have any relation to reality at all. If you are merely a sceptic, you must sooner or later ask yourself the question, 'Why should anything go right; even observation and deduction? Why should not good logic be as misleading as bad logic? They are both movements in the brain of a bewildered ape." Chesterton, *Orthodoxy* (Garden City, NY: Doubleday, 1959), p. 33.

8. Shirley MacLaine, *Going Within: A Guide to Inner Transformation* (New York, NY: Bantam, 1989), p. 262.

9. *Humanist Manifesto II* (Buffalo, NY: Prometheus, 1973), p. 16.

10. Bram Stoker, *Dracula* (New York, NY: Bantam, 1981), p. 200.

11. Chesterton, *Orthodoxy,* p. 150.

12. Ibid.

13. This may seem like a harsh generalization, but only until one considers Romans 1:20: "For since the creation of the world God's invisible qualities—his eternal power and divine nature—have been clearly seen, being understood from what has been made, so that men are without excuse." The atheist knows that God exists, but he has chosen to embrace a comfortable dogma that disallows that existence. His faith in empiricism allows him, ironically, to close his eyes to the empirical evidence of design in nature, which implies a Designer.

14. Don't be shocked to find someone in the Frankenstein crowd denying the existence of free will. As William Kilpatrick points out, "The words sin, repentance, and forgiveness all imply freedom and responsibility. When you take away those labels, you very often take away freedom and responsibility as well." Kilpatrick, *Psychological Seduction* (Nashville, TN: Thomas Nelson, 1983), p. 82.

15. B.F. Skinner, cited in Daniel W. Bjork, *B.F. Skinner: A Life* (New York, NY: Basic, 1993), p. 226.

16. B.F. Skinner, *A Matter of Consequences* (New York, NY: Knopf, 1983), p. 412.

17. Ibid, p. 413.

18. You should be scratching your head at this point. Why would Skinner seek to convince others that he was right, when according to his own theory everyone is determined by their environment to "think" in a certain way? How could argument cause them to "change their minds," if they don't have the freedom to choose to change their minds? If Skinner is to be consistent with his beliefs, he must look at the Christian and conclude, "Unfortunately, you'll always believe in Christianity until your environment causes you to cease to believe. Rather than arguing with you, then, I should seek to change your environment so that it causes you to change." And Skinner did, in fact, say something quite like this: "I am not trying to change people. All I want to do is change the world in which they live" (cited in Bjork, *B.F. Skinner: A Life,* p. 233). Of course, it's tempting to ask Skinner why he is free to change the world when everyone else isn't even free to choose what socks they will wear.

19. B.F. Skinner, *Science and Human Behavior* (New York, NY: Macmillan, 1953), p. 447.

20. B.F. Skinner, *Beyond Freedom and Dignity* (New York, NY: Bantam, 1972), p. 63.

21. Skinner wrote a novel in which the protagonist, Frazier, defends behaviorism and consequently often speaks for Skinner. When Frazier is asked about his beliefs about history, he says that it should be honored only as "entertainment" and not "taken seriously as food for thought." B.F. Skinner, *Walden Two* (New York, NY: Macmillan, 1962), p. 115.

22. Stephen Jay Gould, *Wonderful Life* (New York, NY: W.W. Norton, 1989), p. 24.

23. Kilpatrick, *Psychological Seduction*, p. 47.

24. Certain scientists may take umbrage at the statement that man has never witnessed evolution. These scientists might point to the famed peppered moth or the variation among dog breeds as examples of evolution. Strictly speaking, however, these are at best examples of micro-evolution, and do not in any way demonstrate the controversial aspect of evolutionary theory—the belief that existing species can give rise to new species.

25. G.K. Chesterton, *The Club of Queer Trades* (New York, NY: Penguin, 1984), p. 113.

26. Karl Barth, "Christianity or Religion?" *Fragments Grave and Gay* (Glasgow: William Collins Sons, 1976), p. 30.

27. Phillip Johnson, *Reason in the Balance* (Downers Grove, IL: InterVarsity, 1995), p. 37.

28. Barbara von der Heydt, *Candles Behind the Wall* (Grand Rapids, MI: Eerdmans, 1993), p. 28.

29. Johnson, *Reason in the Balance*, p. 199.

30. Pascal, *Pensees*, p. 83.

31. Skinner, *Walden Two*, p. 193.

32. H.G. Wells, *The Time Machine* (New York, NY: Tor, 1992), p. 39.

33. Dorothy Sayers, *The Mind of the Maker* (San Francisco, CA: Harper Collins, 1979), p. 16.

34. Chesterton, *Orthodoxy*, p. 15.

35. Ibid.

36. Abraham Lincoln, in his October 15, 1858 debate with Stephen Douglas, in Kerner, ed., *A Treasury of Lincoln Quotations*, p. 17.

37. R.C. Sproul, *Reason to Believe* (Grand Rapids, Ml: Zondervan, 1982), p. 99.

38. Pascal, *Pensees*, p. 88.

39. Abraham Maslow, *Toward a Psychology of Being* (New York, NY: Van

Nostrand Reinhold, 1968), p. 6. Muslims, Jews, Mormons and Jehovah's Witnesses, it should be noted, would never make such a blunt assertion, but their conclusion is strikingly similar. Man, for them, has the capacity to work out his own salvation, and he can do so if he can keep himself from being tainted by the temptations and distractions around him.

40. Kilpatrick, *Psychological Seduction*, p. 42.

41. Ibid.

42. Abraham Maslow's February 1, 1969 journal entry, in Richard J. Lowry, ed., *The Journals of A.H. Maslow* (Monterey, CA: Brooks/Cole, 1979), p. 1109.

43. Abraham Maslow, "Preface to the Second Edition," *Motivation and Personality* (New York, NY: Harper & Row, 1970), p. xx.

44. Chesterton, *The Everlasting Man,* p. 12.

45. Robert Muller, *New Genesis: Shaping a Global Spirituality* (Garden City, NY: Doubleday, 1982), pp. 190-191. Muller's reverence for the United Nations is typical of a New Age proponent. Most believers in the New Age expect that national boundaries must be destroyed, and the world must be united before mankind can become fully aware of its godhood.

46. Ibid, p. 191.

47. Dorothy Sayers, "Creed or Chaos?" *The Whimsical Christian* (New York, NY: Macmillan, 1987), pp. 44-45.

48. C.E.M. Joad, *The Recovery of Belief* (London: Faber & Faber, 1955), p. 82.

49. Ibid, p. 59.

50. Ibid, p. 82.

51. Ibid, p. 63.

52. Ibid, p. 64.

53. Ibid, p. 46.

54. Chesterton, "The Eye of Apollo," *The Annotated Innocence of Father Brown* (New York, NY: Oxford University, 1988), p. 199.

55. C.S. Lewis, "On Obstinacy in Belief," *The World's Last Night* (San Diego, CA: Harcourt Brace, 1987), p. 26.

56. Ibid, pp. 23-24.

57. Sayers, "What Do We Believe?" *The Whimsical Christian,* p. 30.

58. Dorothy Sayers, *The Nine Tailors* (New York, NY: Harcourt, Brace & World, 1962), p. 109.

59. Dietrich Bonhoeffer, *Ethics* (New York, NY: Macmillan, 1986), pp. 196-197.

60. Ibid, p. 197.

61. Ibid, p. 201.
62. C.S. Lewis, "Is Theology Poetry?" *The Weight of Glory* (New York, NY: Macmillan, 1980), p. 92.
63. Pascal, *Pensees*, p. 248.
64. Leo Tolstoy, *Anna Karenin* (Baltimore, MD: Penguin, 1971), p. 820.

CHAPTER 3

1. Blaise Pascal, *Pensees* (New York, NY: Penguin, 1986), p. 62.
2. Benjamin Franklin, *The Autobiography and Other Writings* (New York, NY: Signet, 1961), p. 94.
3. Ibid, p. 96.
4. Ibid, p. 94.
5. Ibid.
6. Ibid, p. 99.
7. Ibid, p. 102.
8. Ibid, p. 101.
9. Ibid, pp. 103-104.
10. Dorothy Sayers, "The Other Six Deadly Sins," *The Whimsical Christian* (New York, NY: Macmillan, 1987), p. 177. I would contend, of course, that "perfectibility of man" is the name under which pride has always walked the earth—that every thinking non-Christian has always believed (pridefully) that they could rescue themselves, rather than relying on Christ.
11. William Kilpatrick, *Psychological Seduction* (Nashville, TN: Thomas Nelson, 1983), pp. 36-37.
12. Charles Darwin, in a letter to W. Graham, July 3, 1881, *Life and Letters of Charles Darwin*, ed. F. Darwin (New York, NY: D. Appleton & Co., 1904), vol. 1, p. 286.
13. Shirley MacLaine, *It's All in the Playing* (New York, NY: Bantam, 1987), p. 175.
14. Kilpatrick, *Identity and Intimacy* (New York, NY: Delacorte, 1975), p. 142.
15. Shakti Gawain, *Living in the Light* (San Rafael, CA: New World, 1986), p. 128.
16. Ayn Rand, ed., *The Virtue of Selfishness* (New York, NY: Signet Books, 1964), p. viii. Interestingly, Rand claims on page xi that "The attack on 'selfishness' is an attack on man's self-esteem; to surrender one, is to surrender the other." The following chapter will examine this relationship between the modern self-esteem movement and selfishness.

17. Nathaniel Branden, "Isn't Everyone Selfish?", *The Virtue of Selfishness,* pp. 58-59.

18. Ibid, p. 59.

19. Ibid, p. 60.

20. Ramana Maharshi, *Maharshi's Gospel* (Tiruvannamalai: Sri Ramanasraman, 1949), pp. 33-34.

21. Abraham Maslow, *Toward a Psychology of Being* (New York, NY: Van Nostrand Reinhold, 1968), p. 4.

22. Erich Fromm, *Man for Himself* (New York, NY: Holt, Rinehart and Winston, 1964), pp. 126-127.

23. Catherine Heim, *Colorado Springs Gazette-Telegraph,* May 16, 1996, p. B4.

24. Dietrich Bonhoeffer, *The Cost of Discipleship* (New York, NY: Macmillan, 1963), p. 99.

25. This anecdote is described in Owen Chadwick, *The Secularization of the European Mind in the 19th Century* (New York, NY: Cambridge University, 1990), p. 58.

26. Pascal, *Pensees,* p. 347.

27. B.F. Skinner, *Walden Two* (New York, NY: Macmillan, 1962), p. 300.

28. Ravi Zacharias, *A Shattered Visage: The Real Face of Atheism* (Brentwood, TN: Wolgemuth & Hyatt, 1990), pp. 133-134.

29. Bonhoeffer, *The Cost of Discipleship,* p. 178.

30. C.S. Lewis, *Beyond Personality* (New York, NY: Macmillan, 1947), p. 25.

31. Lewis, *Till We Have Faces* (San Diego, CA: Harcourt Brace, 1956), p. 279.

32. Charles Colson, *Loving God* (Grand Rapids, MI: Zondervan, 1987), p. 25.

33. Lewis, *Beyond Personality,* p. 40.

34. Ibid, p. 41.

35. Lewis, "The Sermon and the Lunch," *God in the Dock* (Grand Rapids, MI: Eerdmans, 1994), p. 286.

36. Sayers, "What Do We Believe?" *The Whimsical Christian,* p. 32.

37. It's interesting to notice here one of the differences between Christian ethics and the highest ethical precept ever articulated by a non-Christian worldview. Some critics of Christianity point out that Christ's Golden Rule was described by other worldview proponents before His birth. Non-Christians like to remind us of this because they believe it demonstrates that Christ's ethical teachings didn't differ significantly from those of other moralists, which in turn is

supposed to demonstrate that Christ was simply a man borrowing teachings from other men. These critics need to remember, however, that non-Christian ethical teachers prescribed at best only a negative formulation of the Golden Rule. Russell Kirk explains, "In its negative form, [the Golden Rule] was stated by Hillel, the great Jewish teacher who lived about Jesus' time: 'Do not do unto others what you would not wish others to do unto you.' It appears thus in other sacred writings of the Jews, and in other religions; in this negative expression, it was a saying of Confucious." *The Roots of American Order* (Washington, DC: Regnery Gateway, 1992), p. 144. A moment's reflection will reveal, however, the extraordinary gulf between a negative and a positive expression of the Golden Rule: one provides only a list of "don'ts," while the other compels men to humble themselves and focus on others more than themselves. One makes morality reactive, the other proactive. Put simply, the negative version says "Live and let live," while the positive version requires you to die to yourself.

38. G.K. Chesterton, *What's Wrong with the World* (San Francisco, CA: Ignatius, 1994), p. 37.
39. "Perspectives," *Newsweek*, September 6, 1993, p. 13.
40. Doug Nichols, "What Seminary Can't Teach," *World*, March 12, 1994, p. 26.
41. Max Hocutt, "Toward an Ethic of Mutual Accommodation," *Humanist Ethics*, ed. Morris B. Storer (Buffalo, NY: Prometheus, 1980), p. 138.
42. *Humanist Manifesto II* (Buffalo, NY: Prometheus, 1973), p. 17.
43. M. Russell Ballard, one of the Twelve Apostles overseeing the Mormon church, writes, "[W]e are also aware that the Bible has been through countless translations from the time its chapters were originally penned to the present. Along the way there have been changes and alterations that have diminished the purity of the doctrine. While it is indeed a miracle that the Bible has survived through the ages at all, it would be unreasonable to assume that it has done so completely intact" *Our Search for Happiness* (Salt Lake City, UT: Deseret, 1993), p. 95.
44. Kilpatrick, *Psychological Seduction*, p. 53.
45. Marxists certainly view ethics this way, because they look forward to a world when all the morality of the property owners will have been eradicated, right along with the property owners. As V.I. Lenin says, "If war is waged by the proletariat [the working class] after it has

conquered the bourgeoisie [the property owners] in its own country, and is waged with the object of strengthening and developing socialism, such a war is legitimate and 'holy'" *Collected Works* (Moscow: Progress, 1977), vol. 27, p. 332. Ethics, for the Marxist, are determined by a country's economic system, and so when the economic system changes the new people in power get to determine what is right and what is wrong.

46. Marianne Williamson, *A Woman's Worth* (New York, NY: Random House, 1993), p. 106.
47. Dr. Seuss, "The Zax," *The Sneetches and Other Stories* (New York, NY: Random House, 1989), pp. 27-28.
48. Ibid, p. 32.
49. Ibid, p. 35.
50. Colson, *Against the Night* (Ann Arbor, MI: Servant, 1989), p. 47.
51. H.R. Rookmaaker, *Modern Art and the Death of a Culture* (Wheaton, IL: Crossway, 1994), pp. 246-247.
52. For a full account of this debacle, see Bob Jones IV, "Creating Controversy," *World,* January 25, 1997, p. 18.
53. Feminist and New Age proponent Gloria Steinem writes, "There is always one true inner voice. Trust it." *Revolution from Within* (Boston, MA: Little, Brown & Co., 1992), p. 323.
54. Pascal, *Pensees,* p. 60.
55. Alexander Solzhenitsyn, *The Gulag Archipelago* (New York, NY: Harper & Row, 1974), p. 160.
56. Lewis, "The World's Last Night," *The World's Last Night* (San Diego, CA: Harcourt Brace, 1987), p. 106.
57. Ibid, pp. 104-105.

CHAPTER 4

1. Robert Louis Stevenson, *Dr. Jekyll and Mr. Hyde* (New York, NY: Bantam, 1981), p. 83.
2. Neil J. Smelser, "Self-Esteem and Social Problems: An Introduction" in eds. Andrew M. Mecca, Neil J. Smelser, and John Vasconcellos, *The Social Importance of Self-Esteem* (Berkeley, CA: University of California, 1989), p. 1.
3. Andrew M. Mecca, "Foreword," in Ibid, p. vii.
4. Shirley MacLaine, in Robert W. Butler, "MacLaine's Ideas Almost Mainstream Now, She Says," *The Denver Post,* March 21, 1994, p. 1E.
5. John Vasconcellos, "Preface," *The Social Importance of Self-Esteem,* p. xii.

6. "The Family, Teenage Pregnancy, Child Abuse, and Self-esteem," *Toward a State of Esteem: The Final Report of the California Task Force to Promote Self-esteem and Personal and Social Responsibility* (Sacramento, CA: California Department of Education, 1990), p. 45.

7. Humanist author Wendell W. Watters insists that even the most lukewarm Christians believe things that "could have side effects that are deleterious to their mental health and that of their children" Watters, "Christianity and Mental Health," *The Humanist,* Nov/Dec 1987, p. 5.

8. Jerry Adler, "Hey, I'm Terrific!" *Newsweek,* February 17, 1992, p. 51.

9. Stephen Jay Gould, *Wonderful Life: The Burgess Shale and the Nature of History* (New York, NY: W.W. Norton, 1989), p. 44.

10. Marianne Williamson, *A Return to Love* (New York, NY: HarperCollins, 1992), p. 209.

11. Ibid, p. 208.

12. Ibid.

13. Ibid, p. 209.

14. Ibid, p. 210.

15. Ibid, p. 212.

16. Williamson really believes that the AIDS virus can be converted back into a positive energy in people's lives. On page 209 she puts it this way: "Disease is love turned into fear—our own energy, meant to sustain us, turned against ourselves. Energy cannot be destroyed. Our job is not to kill disease, but to turn its energy back in the direction it came from—to turn fear back into love."

17. Shakti Gawain, *Living in the Light* (San Rafael, CA: New World Library, 1986), p. 156.

18. William Kilpatrick, *Psychological Seduction* (Nashville, TN: Thomas Nelson, 1983), pp. 21-22.

19. Williamson, *A Return to Love,* p. 235.

20. Ibid, p. 239. Williamson's sloppy use of scripture is especially appalling here, since she conveniently omits the first part of John 16:33, where Christ promises that "In this world you will have trouble . . ." The message of this verse is exactly the opposite of Williamson's interpretation. Instead of promising an earthly paradise, Christ is explaining that men can expect to suffer and occasionally be unhappy on earth, but His death and resurrection ensure His followers a better life with Him after we leave this world.

21. Peter Kreeft, *The Angel and the Ants* (Ann Arbor, MI: Servant, 1994), p. 173.

22. Kilpatrick, *Psychological Seduction,* p. 37.

23. Ibid, pp. 15-16.

24. Ibid, p. 14.

25. Abraham Maslow, in a May 5, 1968 journal entry, in Richard J. Lowry, ed., *The Journals of A.H. Maslow* (Monterey, CA: Brooks/Cole, 1979), p. 919.

26. Sigmund Freud, cited in E. Fuller Torrey, *Freudian Fraud* (New York, NY: HarperCollins, 1992), p. 243.

27. Kilpatrick, *Psychological Seduction,* p. 29.

28. Ibid, p. 177.

29. C.S. Lewis, "The Humanitarian Theory of Punishment," *God in the Dock* (Grand Rapids, MI: William B. Eerdmans, 1994), p. 294.

30. Jay Adams, *The Biblical View of Self-Esteem, Self-Love, Self-Image* (Eugene, OR: Harvest House, 1986), p. 105.

31. Lewis, *The Problem of Pain* (New York, NY: Macmillan, 1962), p. 42.

32. David Meyers, *The Inflated Self* (New York, NY: Seabury, 1981), pp. 23-24.

33. Jerry Adler, "Hey, I'm Terrific!" p. 46.

34. Ibid, p. 48.

35. Ibid, p. 51.

36. Smelser, "Self-Esteem and Social Problems: An Introduction," p. 15.

37. Kilpatrick, *Psychological Seduction,* p. 37.

38. Stevenson, *Dr. Jekyll and Mr. Hyde,* p. 20.

39. Kilpatrick, *Psychological Seduction,* p. 61.

40. Blaise Pascal, *Pensees* (New York, NY: Penguin, 1986), p. 95.

41. Kilpatrick, *Psychological Seduction,* p. 191.

42. Francis A. Schaeffer, "True Spirituality," in Th*e Complete Works of Francis Schaeffer* (Westchester, IL: Crossway, 1982), vol. 3, p. 322.

43. Kilpatrick, *Psychological Seduction,* p. 181.

44. Ibid, p. 185.

45. Dorothy Sayers, "Creed or Chaos?" *The Whimsical Christian* (New York, NY: Macmillan, 1987), p. 44.

46. Kilpatrick, *Psychological Seduction,* p. 181.

47. There is a certain irony in the non-Christian's pursuit of happiness, since practicing the virtue of selfishness makes happiness especially difficult to attain. Kilpatrick writes on page 62 of *Psychological Seduction* that "an emphasis on self-awareness, a common prescription for happiness, is often self-defeating. Happiness comes more frequently when attention is focused outside the self."

48. Whittaker Chambers, *Witness* (South Bend, IN: Regnery Gateway, 1979), p. 85.

49. Dietrich Bonhoeffer, *The Cost of Discipleship* (New York, NY: Macmillan, 1963), p. 201.
50. Sayers, "Creed or Chaos?" p. 46.
51. Kilpatrick, *Psychological Seduction*, p. 189.
52. Viktor Frankl, *Man's Search for Meaning* (New York, NY: Washington Square, 1963), p. 106.
53. Ibid, p. 104.
54. Ibid, p. 175.
55. Ibid, p. 122.
56. Schaeffer, *True Spirituality*, p. 330.
57. Kilpatrick, *Psychological Seduction*, p. 66.
58. Ibid, p. 72.
59. Ibid, p. 67.
60. Mary Shelley, *Frankenstein* (New York, NY: Bantam, 1981), p. 204.
61. Scott Montgomery, "Don't Blame Me!" *Colorado Springs Gazette-Telegraph,* January 22, 1995, p. D1. McDonald's appealed the jury's decision, and later settled with Liebeck for an undisclosed sum.
62. Ibid.
63. Jimmy Carter, "Interview with the National Black Network," *Weekly Compilation of Presidential Documents,* July 1977.
64. Lewis, *The Case for Christianity* (New York, NY: Macmillan, 1989), p. 7.
65. Kilpatrick, *Psychological Seduction*, p. 83.
66. Someone may object here that they know non-Christians who believe a lot of the same things that Christians believe. This does not, however, demonstrate the similarity between Christianity and other worldviews, but only the fact that non-Christians must import Christian concepts into their worldviews to be able to function in reality. The non-Christian use of Christian concepts makes them less consistent with their own worldview, but more consistent with the facts of real life.
67. Kilpatrick, *Psychological Seduction*, pp. 70-71.

CHAPTER 5

1. T.S. Eliot, *The Rock* (London: Faber & Faber, 1934), p. 42.
2. Margaret Sanger, *The Pivot of Civilization* (New York, NY: Brentano's, 1922), p. 115. George Grant's excellent work *Grand Illusions* provides a much more complete portrait of Sanger's life and legacy.
3. Ibid, pp. 116-117.
4. Ibid, p. 96.

5. George Grant, *Grand Illusions* (Brentwood, TN: Wolgemuth & Hyatt, 1988), p. 57.
6. Ian Taylor, *In the Minds of Men* (Toronto: TFE, 1991), p. 408.
7. Grant, *Grand Illusions*, p. 63.
8. Carl Rogers, "Notes on Rollo May," *Journal of Humanistic Psychology,* Summer 1982, p. 8.
9. Abraham Maslow, *Toward a Psychology of Being* (New York, NY: Van Nostrand Reinhold, 1968), p. 6.
10. B.F. Skinner, *Walden Two* (New York, NY: Macmillan, 1962), p. 273.
11. Skinner, *Science and Human Behavior* (New York, NY: Macmillan, 1953), p. 6.
12. Ivan Pavlov, *Conditioned Reflexes and Psychiatry* (New York, NY: International, 1963), p. 144.
13. Skinner, *Beyond Freedom and Dignity* (New York, NY: Bantam, 1972), p. 63.
14. The behaviorist denies the existence of free will, so it seems strange to expect anyone to be able to choose to change the environment that determines their behavior. The consistent atheist must admit that he can never change the environment unless the environment forces him to change it. Why, then, would behaviorists seek to persuade people to do something they will either be forced or forbidden to do?
15. Shakti Gawain, *Living in the Light* (San Rafael, CA: New World, 1986), p. 110.
16. Horace Mann, "Introduction," *The Common School Journal,* January 1, 1841, p. 15.
17. Neil J. Smelser, "Self-Esteem and Social Problems: An Introduction," *The Social Importance of Self-Esteem,* eds. Andrew M. Mecca, Neil J. Smelser, and John Vasconcellos (Berkeley, CA: University of California, 1989), pp. 1-2.
18. Skinner, in an interview with Tom Fitzpatrick, *Chicago Sun Tribune,* March 29, 1972, p. 24.
19. Skinner, *Walden Two*, p. 231.
20. Taylor, *In the Minds of Men,* p. 410.
21. *World* magazine reported in their September 21, 1996 issue that "Classroom teachers are outnumbered by other public education employees by a ratio of 3-to-2" (p. 9).
22. *World,* September 14, 1996, p. 7.
23. Roy Maynard, "How to Teach Young Dogs Some Old Tricks," *World,* February 22, 1997, p. 19.
24. Dietrich Bonhoeffer, *Ethics* (New York, NY: Macmillan, 1986), p. 107.

25. Russell Kirk, *The Roots of American Order* (Washington, DC: Regnery Gateway, 1992), p. 189.

26. Alexander Solzhenitsyn, *The Gulag Archipelago* (New York, NY: Harper & Row, 1974), p. 101.

27. Fyodor Dostoyevsky, *The Devils* (New York, NY: Penguin, 1971), p. 405.

28. Skinner, *Walden Two*, p. 297.

29. Voltaire, cited in Owen Chadwick, *The Secularization of the European Mind in the 19th Century* (New York, NY: Cambridge University, 1990), p. 10.

30. Corliss Lamont, *The Philosophy of Humanism* (New York, NY: Frederick Ungar, 1982), p. 248.

31. Sigmund Freud, cited in E. Fuller Torrey, *Freudian Fraud* (New York, NY: HarperCollins, 1992), pp. 242-243.

32. Benjamin Franklin, *The Autobiography and Other Writings* (New York, NY: Signet, 1961), p. 106.

33. Ginger Pace, "No Thanks," *World,* February 22, 1997, p. 26.

34. Skinner, *Walden Two,* p. 142.

35. Janet Reno, cited in William Norman Grigg, "Whose Child is This?" *The New American,* November 28, 1994, p. 23.

36. Jack Westman, cited in Ibid.

37. G.K. Chesterton, *Orthodoxy* (Garden City, NY: Doubleday, 1959), p. 141.

38. Ibid, p. 118.

39. Ibid, p. 117.

40. Ibid, p. 141.

41. Barbara von der Heydt, *Candles Behind the Wall* (Grand Rapids, MI: William B. Eerdmans, 1993), p. xix.

42. Calvin Coolidge, in an address to the Massachusetts Senate, in William Safire, ed., *Lend Me Your Ears* (New York, NY: W.W. Norton, 1992), p. 56.

43. Bonhoeffer, *Ethics,* p. 164.

44. Ibid, p. 104.

45. Kirk, *The Roots of American Order,* p. 29.

46. James Madison, "Number 51," *The Federalist Papers* (New York, NY: Simon & Schuster, 1964), pp. 122-123.

47. Kirk, *The Roots of American Order,* p. 29.

48. Chesterton, *Orthodoxy,* p. 119.

49. Bonhoeffer, *Ethics,* p. 102.

50. Edmund Burke, "A Letter to a Member of the National Assembly," *Further Reflections on the Revolution in France* (Indianapolis, IN:

Liberty Fund, 1992), p. 69.

51. Alexis de Tocqueville, *Democracy in America* (New York, NY: Knopf, 1948), vol. 1, p. 307.

52. Von der Heydt, *Candles Behind the Wall,* p. 254.

53. Coolidge, in Safire, ed., *Lend Me Your Ears,* p. 55.

54. Bonhoeffer, *Ethics,* p. 207.

55. Roy Maynard, "Colorado Voters Ask: Whose Kids are They?" *World,* October 26, 1996, p. 17.

56. William Kilpatrick, *Psychological Seduction* (Nashville, TN: Thomas Nelson, 1983), p. 127.

57. Lord Melbourne, cited in Charles Colson, *Kingdoms in Conflict* (Grand Rapids, MI: Zondervan, 1987), p. 101.

58. Bonhoeffer, *Ethics,* p. 153.

59. Lewis, "Man or Rabbit?" *God in the Dock* (Grand Rapids, MI: William B. Eerdmans, 1994), p. 110.

60. Dorothy Sayers, *The Unpleasantness at the Bellona Club* (New York, NY: HarperCollins, 1993), p. 215.

61. Solzhenitsyn, *The Gulag Archipelago,* p. 174.

62. William Goulding, *Lord of the Flies* (New York, NY: Capricorn, 1959), p. 49.

CHAPTER 6

1. G.K. Chesterton, *The Club of Queer Trades* (New York, NY: Penguin, 1984), p. 31.

2. Lord Byron, cited in Gyles Brandreth, ed., *Famous Last Words and Tombstone Humor* (New York, NY: Sterling, 1989), p. 10.

3. G.K. Chesterton, in Ibid, p. 21.

4. William Kilpatrick, *Psychological Seduction* (Nashville, TN: Thomas Nelson, 1983), pp. 234-235.

5. C.S. Lewis, *Beyond Personality* (New York, NY: Macmillan, 1947), p. 48.

6. Ibid, p. 67.

7. Karl Barth, *Dogmatics in Outline* (New York, NY: Harper & Row, 1959), p. 25.

8. Blaise Pascal, *Pensees* (New York, NY: Penguin, 1986), p. 133.

9. Chesterton, *The Everlasting Man* (Garden City, NY: Doubleday, 1955), p. 27.

10. Russell Kirk, *The Roots of American Order* (Washington, DC: Regnery Gateway, 1992), p. 146.

11. B.F. Skinner, *Walden Two* (New York, NY: Macmillan, 1962), p. 234.

12. Dietrich Bonhoeffer, *The Cost of Discipleship* (New York, NY: Macmillan, 1963), p. 97.

13. Ibid, p. 211.

14. Sir Thomas Browne, "Christian Morals," *The Works of Sir Thomas Browne*, ed. Charles Sayle (Edinburg: John Grant, 1927), p. 449.

15. George Roche, *A World Without Heroes* (Hillsdale, MI: Hillsdale College, 1987), p. xii.

16. Alexander Solzhenitsyn, *The Gulag Archipelago* (New York, NY: Harper & Row, 1974), p. 17.

17. Kilpatrick, *Why Johnny Can't Tell Right from Wrong* (New York, NY: Simon & Schuster, 1992), p. 86.

18. Ibid, p. 18.

19. If Christians fail to model righteousness, our children will readily seek out others to be their role models. In America, the most popular alternative role models are pop icons, who model behavior for the next generation via television, movies, music, etc. Marilyn Manson, one of the most anti-God rock stars in history, recognizes this and warns, "Raise your kids better or I'll raise them for you" (*World,* November 16, 1996, p. 23).

20. Robert Louis Stevenson, *Dr. Jekyll and Mr. Hyde* (New York, NY: Bantam, 1981), pp. 93-94.

21. Kilpatrick, *Why Johnny Can't Tell Right from Wrong,* p. 200.

22. Ibid, p. 201.

23. C.E.M. Joad, *The Recovery of Belief* (London: Faber & Faber, 1955), pp. 65-66.

24. Kilpatrick, *Psychological Seduction,* p. 231.

25. Paul Attner, "Complete Success," *The Sporting News,* August 23, 1993, p. S-3.

26. As noted earlier, none of this is meant to downplay the importance of speaking up for Christ. Christians are compelled to acknowledge their faith and be prepared to defend it, verbally. But our words will only be credible if they are consistent with our actions.

27. Barbara von der Heydt, *Candles Behind the Wall* (Grand Rapids, MI: Eerdmans, 1993), p. 30.

28. Cited in Joe Maxwell, "Reversing Roe One Heart at a Time," *World,* January 13, 1996, p. 14.

29. H.G. Wells, *The Invisible Man* (New York, NY: Airmont, 1964), p. 133.

30. Barth, "Atheism, For and Against," *Fragments Grave and Gay* (Glasgow: William Collins Sons, 1976), pp. 43-44.

31. Chesterton, *The Everlasting Man,* p. 237.

32. Bonhoeffer, *Ethics* (New York, NY: Macmillan, 1986), p. 225.

To find more biblical discussions about
great books, visit www.TheGreatBooks.com.